Dear Old Blighty

Britain's First World War Home Front

"Drinking is pre-judicial to victory."
—*Lord Roberts.*

" Abstinence is necessary for the highest efficiency,"
—*Admiral Jellicoe.*

" We have to fight three enemies—the Germans, the Austrians and Drink—but **the greatest of these is Drink**."—*Chancellor of the Exchequer.*

PATRIOTIC PLEDGE:

In order that I may be of the greatest Service to my Country at this time of national peril **I Promise** by God's help to abstain from all intoxicants until the end of the war, and to encourage others to do the same.

Name *David Thomas*

Address *3, Nicholl St*

Published by   *Watkins' Ltd., Swansea.*

Dear Old Blighty

Britain's First World War
Home Front

Mike Brown

SABRESTORM

Designed and typeset by Philip Clucas MSIAD

British Library Cataloguing in Publication Data

A catalogue record for this book is available from
the British Library

Published by Sabrestorm Publishing,
The Olive Branch, Caen Hill, Devizes SN10 1RB
Website: www.sabrestorm.com
Email: books@sabrestorm.com

Printed in Malaysia by Tien Wah Press

ISBN: 9781781220108

Contents

Introduction

Opposite page 'Absent friends', an illustration from 1915. The fact that 'Daddy' is an officer shows that this is a fairly affluent family. However, for most celebrating Christmas 1915 the meal would have been simpler, and held in far plainer surroundings.

In the summer of 1914, Britain and her colonies were basking, not only in the sun, but also at being part of the greatest Empire in history. The divides between rich and poor were huge, yet most of the working class enjoyed a standard of living higher than that of their forebears. For most, the feeling was one of certainty; Britain's place in the world order was secure, and her citizens' lifestyles equally assured.

The nineteenth century had seen the industrial revolution at its height. It began in the British textile industry, and saw production expand hugely as Richard Arkwright and others developed machines which sped up production and also required little skill to use. These developments led to the idea of factories, which in turn utilised the new power source, steam, to run more and ever-bigger machines, leading to mass-production.

These new products had to be taken to their markets, and the steam engine developed into the train, which transported coal and raw materials to the factories, and took their products to the population centres. Rapid expansion of production called for new markets abroad, and the ports expanded, filling up with steam ships which carried products across the world, returning with exotic goods and raw materials.

Improvements in farming cut down the number of workers needed on the land, freeing them to work in the factories. For every person in the UK in 1800, there were almost four by 1914. This boom in population soon outstripped our farmers' ability to feed the country. Imports filled the gap, and the Royal Navy, the greatest in the world, protected our merchantmen.

Britain was not the only country experiencing industrialisation, other countries, too were seeking global markets. The easiest answer was the 'captive market', where a country had no choice but to buy your products, and supply your raw materials. These would be countries which had become colonies; part of the British, French, or other empire.

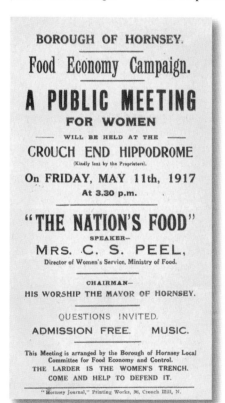

BOROUGH OF HORNSEY.

Food Economy Campaign.

A PUBLIC MEETING
FOR WOMEN
—— WILL BE HELD AT THE ——
CROUCH END HIPPODROME
(Kindly lent by the Proprietors).

On FRIDAY, MAY 11th, 1917
At 3.30 p.m.

"THE NATION'S FOOD"
SPEAKER—
MRS. C. S. PEEL,
Director of Women's Service, Ministry of Food.

CHAIRMAN—
HIS WORSHIP THE MAYOR OF HORNSEY.

QUESTIONS INVITED.
ADMISSION FREE.   MUSIC.

This Meeting is arranged by the Borough of Hornsey Local Committee for Food Economy and Control.
THE LARDER IS THE WOMEN'S TRENCH.
COME AND HELP TO DEFEND IT.

"Hornsey Journal," Printing Works, 36, Crouch Hill, N.

Above Our reliance on imported food would prove a weakness the German U-Boats would try to take advantage of.

Right David Lloyd George, 'the Welsh Wizard'. When war broke out he was Chancellor of the Exchequer in Asquith's Liberal government, becoming Minister of Munitions in May 1915, Secretary of State for War in June 1916, and Prime Minister that December.

THE RIGHT HON·
D·LLOYD GEORGE

Over the course of the nineteenth century, European empires hugely expanded; at the beginning of the period the map of Africa shows a few isolated enclaves of Empire, by 1870, little of the continent that had not been gobbled up.

For the industrialised countries, this pattern of expansion and increased profits seemed endless. At first, there seemed to be plenty of new land, but as empires grew, they began to clash over disputed territories. These clashes led to treaties and alliances, which formed power blocks which seemed to equal each other out. The stresses were not only between empires but also within them; the move to the cities had destroyed age-old links between farm workers and landowners. The new urban working class owed little loyalty to their new bosses, leading to a rise in trades unions and worker-based political movements. As with all finely-balanced systems the result seemed strong, yet, as events would show, a single unforeseen event could bring the entire thing tumbling down.

The War, when it came, was industrialised. Factories clothed and armed soldiers in undreamed of numbers and trains and ships transported them over vast distances. Industry produced new weapons: dreadnoughts, aircraft, submarines, tanks and poison gas. There had never been a war like it, and not only on the battlefields; but also on the home front.

In Britain the war would need millions of male civilians to become servicemen, first through volunteering, later by conscription. At the same time industry expanded to produce the munitions needed by the ever-expanding armies and navies. To do this, women workers were progressively required to replace the men going to the front, not only in the factories but in transport, offices, and a host of other jobs. Children, too had their part to play, either individually, or through organisations such as the Boy Scouts, Girl Guides, etc., or through their schools.

Our lack of self-sufficiency in food was exacerbated as the German Navy, through its U-Boat (submarine) fleet, declared the seas around Britain under blockade; any merchant ship entering the area would be likely to be attacked. Losses of ships, and their precious cargoes, hit civilians hard, leading to shortages, price rises, food queues, and eventually, rationing.

Attacks on coastal towns by German shipping began early in the war, but these were nothing new. Most shocking of all were the attacks on Britain from the air; civilians came under threat, first from Zeppelin attack, then by aeroplanes. Bombing came to Britain at Christmas 1914, the first deaths following soon after in January 1915. The next few years would see the authorities struggling to counter this new threat to the civil population, through anti-aircraft guns, balloons, warnings, etc.,

Many of the ideas brought in, national registration, rationing, the women's land army, the Observer Corps, the blackout and other anti-aircraft measures, have become famous as part of the second world war, but here we see their inception, trials and improvements, so that in 1939 the greater part of these schemes had already been developed.

In this book we examine a rarely-looked at, yet important facet of Britain's experience in World War 1 – the civilian home front.

Chapter 1

The Outbreak of War

Left Field Marshal Horatio Herbert Kitchener, became Secretary of State for War at the start of the conflict. Almost uniquely at that point, he predicted that the war might last three years.

On 28 June 1914, when the Austro-Hungarian Archduke Franz Ferdinand and Archduchess Sophie were assassinated at Sarajevo, people in Britain viewed it as the sort of shocking event that might be expected of foreigners in faraway places. The excitement soon died away and people planned their summer holidays; the wealthy typically went first to Cowes and then on to Scotland; the middle classes went on continental tours or pleasure cruises, and the better-off workers visited seaside resorts around the UK. Few saw events in Europe as any threat to Britain.

Beach North of Britannia Pier, Gt. Yarmouth

Right This postcard was sent from Great Yarmouth on Bank Holiday Monday, 3 August 1914; next day we would be at war!

One month later, on 28 July, Austria declared war on Serbia. European stock exchanges were hit hard as nervous traders tried to sell, and prices plummeted. Within a day, seven firms on the London Stock Exchange could not make payments.

On the 30th July, Russia – Serbia's ally -- mobilised its army; Germany responded, giving Russia just twelve hours to demobilise. In London the Bank of England doubled the official rate of interest from 4 to 8% to steady the market, but to little effect; at 10 am, the London Stock Exchange closed to avoid a financial crash.

Next day, Germany declared war on Russia; France, bound by treaty, mobilised. In Britain, the bank rate rose to 10%; queues formed outside the Bank of England as people franticly tried to change their banknotes into gold.

Below The Anglo American Exposition was a great attraction at London's White City in the summer of 1914, running from 15 May to 26 September 1914. This postcard was sent on 30 July.

On Sunday, Britain mobilised its fleet and called out the naval reserve. Yet many were still setting off on holiday. In 1920, 'Croydon and the Great War', the town's official history, said; *'we believed that by some means or other Sir Edward Grey would accomplish the usual miracle, and keep us and Europe out of war.'*

A meeting was held in Trafalgar Square in support of peace, but it was taken over by government supporters, and passed a motion of support for the government. Large crowds marched to Buckingham Palace singing patriotic songs, and cheering wildly as the King and Queen appeared on the balcony.

The Cascade, Anglo American Exposition, 1914

On Bank Holiday Monday, 3 August, Germany declared war on France and invaded Luxemburg. The German government demanded that their troops be allowed to pass through Belgium, to invade France. The Belgian King, Albert, replied; *'We are a nation, not a road!'*, but German troops marched in anyway. In Britain, it was announced that the stock exchange would remain closed until Friday. A shortage of gold meant that £1 and 10s notes were issued instead, but some shops refused to accept them.

The 1839 Treaty of London required Belgium to remain neutral; the signatories, including Britain, France, and Prussia, were committed to defend that neutrality. Consequently, King Albert appealed to Britain for aid. On Tuesday 4th, Britain responded,

RT. HON. SIR EDWARD GREY, BT., M.P.

PHOTO BY SPEAIGHT. LTD. 157. NEW BOND ST. W. H.M. THE KING OF THE BELGIANS. 99.D. BEAGLES' POSTCARDS

Above left Sir Edward Grey, British Foreign Secretary from 1905 to 1916. The day before we declared war he is reported to have said *"The lamps are going out all over Europe. We shall not see them lit again in our time."*

Above right King Albert of the Belgians, in military uniform, but significantly field uniform, not an ornate dress uniform.

sending its own ultimatum, demanding German withdrawal. Germany ignored the ultimatum, and Britain declared war. Late editions of the evening papers were bought as fast as they appeared; the country was willing to believe the most absurd rumours, such as Russian troops marching through Britain – still with snow on their boots!

The government immediately took control of the railways so that the lines, locomotives, rolling stock and staff could be used to move troops, stores, and food supplies.

On 6 August Lord Kitchener, newly-appointed Secretary of State for War, asked for 500,000 recruits. In the book 'Crieff in the Great War' Andrew Gardiner said, *'it was the belief of many that the war would be over by Christmas time, and not a few stood aghast when Lord Kitchener warned us that it might last three years.'*

The banks reopened on Friday, 7 August, so workers could be paid their wages. There was no fresh run -- but the banks now had the power to refuse payment, and used it when people tried to withdraw large sums.

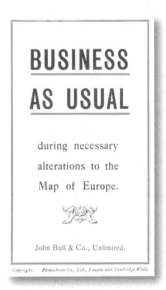

BUSINESS
AS USUAL

during necessary

alterations to the

Map of Europe.

John Bull & Co., Unlimited.

Copyright.   Photochrom Co., Ltd., London and Tunbridge Wells.

Above Many in the business community insisted that it was the duty of civilians to carry on shopping as normal – 'Business as usual' became their catch-phrase, but events proved them woefully wrong.

Across the country, people bought large stocks of preserved foods, expecting food shortages. Many provisions sold out; some shopkeepers tried to meet this rush by supplying only regular customers with their usual quantities, while others raised prices. The day after war was declared, the price of butter rose by almost 30%. The Cabinet set a maximum price for certain staple foods, such as sugar, butter, cheese, lard, bacon, and margarine. The Government bought a huge quantity of sugar -- enough to supply the nation for many months - to be sold at a reasonable price, and issued lists of maximum prices that could be charged for everyday commodities. A notice appeared in some shop windows stating "business as usual", but this campaign soon faded as the realities of war struck home.

Deep uncertainty affected Britain. People stopped buying luxury goods, and public entertainments were cancelled. Thousands of shorthand typists and general assistants were thrown out of work by the closure of offices. Some factories went on half time; some shut altogether. However, when arrangements began to be made for arming, clothing, and equipping Kitchener's half million-strong army, the Yorkshire mills could not produce all the khaki cloth needed for uniforms, Sheffield armaments could not make all the guns required, nor could the Birmingham factories meet the orders for small arms. Firms that had never done military work transformed their plant. At first, firms sought government work, then the government came to them with directions as to what they were to turn out; under the Defence of the Realm Act (DORA), the military authorities could demand all or part of any factory or workshop's products for military supplies, and take over any business they required. DORA also introduced new offences and laws under which civilians could be tried by court martial (military court). These included communicating with the enemy, spreading false reports or reports likely to cause disloyalty, helping the enemy or endangering the war effort.

Throughout the war many people were convinced that Germany would attempt an invasion. This was especially true during the first weeks of war, when nearly all the regular army, including the Territorials (reserves), were sent to France. On several occasions rumours spread that the German fleet had left its home ports. The Home Office drew up procedures to be followed in an invasion; in threatened districts local Emergency Committees were appointed to oversee orderly evacuation, while farmers were told what they must do with their livestock, vehicles, etc. to prevent the invaders seizing them.

Above Boy Scouts guarding a railway line and culvert in September 1914, at the height of the invasion scare.

Unofficial local anti-invasion groups were formed, with names such as 'The City Guards of Bradford', 'The Kent Volunteer Fencibles', and the 'Hinckley Home Defence Corps'. These groups, often organised by former Army officers, armed themselves with sporting guns and other weapons. Some even had unit badges, and a uniform of sorts. Groups such as the 'East Kent Mounted Scouts' were formed around members of the local hunt; others, including the 'Croydon Riflemen', were formed from rifle clubs, while the Second Hull Volunteer Battalion was largely made up of members of the city's golf club.

The Boy Scouts got involved; in Croydon that August two mixed patrols of Scouts assisted the military by patrolling the Kent coast, while 21 senior Scouts guarded South Croydon Station and the adjacent bridges. The railways were seen as a prime target; guards were stationed at bridges, signal boxes and other vulnerable points. Other volunteer sentries took up positions at water reservoirs, gas and electricity works and similar places.

For years Germans had settled here; now people living in Britain but born abroad were seen as possible enemies. Many waiters, butchers and bakers were German. Some were naturalized, many more not. A few hours after war broke out Reginald McKenna, the Home Secretary, issued a notice allowing Germans to leave the UK during the next six days. Those staying in Britain were ordered to register, and regulations limiting their travel were introduced. Some Germans and Austrians tried to change their names, but this was forbidden.

Espionage was made a military offence, punishable by death; a number of Germans suspected of spying were arrested, and a further 200 placed under surveillance. All wireless transmitters in private hands were seized. A bill enabling local authorities to control the movements of 'undesirable aliens' was passed; they were also given power to commandeer any boats. Flying aircraft

Right Belgium refused to allow Germany free passage through their country. The tiny Belgian army could not hope to beat overwhelming odds, but their dogged resistance held the Germans long enough to thwart the surprise attack on Paris.

of any kind over the United Kingdom was banned. Aliens were not allowed to keep carrier pigeons, photographic apparatus, or weapons. The houses of Germans and Austrians were searched, and 9,000 Germans and Austrians of military age, were arrested and confined as prisoners of war. This rose to a peak of 19,000, although many were later released.

Soldiers guarded railway stations, bridges, and water and lighting works, and special constables were enrolled to help regular police carry out their new war duties, and to replace policemen who had volunteered for military service, or been recalled to the army.

HATS OFF !!

At first, people in the Labour movement, many of whom were against the Imperial Russian regime, believed strongly that the UK should not go to war in support of Russia, but once war was declared, agreed it must be won. Trade unions fell into line, agreeing on an industrial truce until the war was over. Thus, on 3 September the TUC called on trade unionists to join the army. They assumed, like many others, that the conflict would be 'over by Christmas'. The industrial truce did not last; by February 1915 there were widespread strikes among shipbuilders and munitions workers on the Clyde. The militant women's suffrage groups also decided that this was no time to pursue their aims, and the government released all those suffragettes convicted of damage to property.

Left Not Everyone agreed with the war. Ramsay MacDonald, Chairman of the Labour Party in 1914, opposed his party's support for the conflict and resigned the party chairmanship.

Chapter 2

Recruitment

Above Herbert Henry Asquith, Liberal Prime Minister from 1908 to 1916

On 7 August, Prime Minister Asquith announced that between 250,000 and 300,000 men had volunteered; within a week parliament voted for a further 500,000, bringing the army's strength up to 1.2 million. So many naval reservists poured in that within a week every ship was fully manned, and naval recruitment was halted for three months.

Alone among the fighting nations, Britain did not have conscription; the government was proud of this. In October 1914 Chancellor Lloyd George declared; "*A volunteer army of fifty thousand is just as good as a forced army of two hundred and fifty thousand.*"

Recruiting

A huge army was needed; on 7 August, Kitchener urged men aged between 19 and 30 to volunteer. Local recruiting committees and public meetings were organised. Signs saying, 'TO THE RECRUITING OFFICE' sprang up, as did posters including the famous 'Kitchener wants You' example.

Despite Kitchener's 19 to 30 age range, proof of age was rarely demanded. Men aged 45+ said that they were thirty, teenage boys were asked their age, and if they replied truthfully that they were under 18, they might be told; '*Come back tomorrow when you're nineteen*'.

Appeals for recruits were made from church pulpits, while theatre, music hall and cinema audiences would see messages such as 'Your King And Country Need You!'.

Right London County Council Tram Tickets in the early part of the war often had adverts or messages on the back, such as this one exhorting men to join the forces.

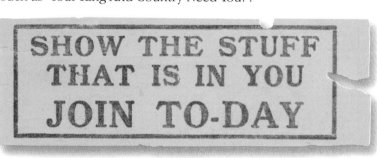

The campaign was very successful; an average of 33,000 men joined every day. Recruiting offices proved totally inadequate to cope with the numbers coming forward. Britain was not prepared for equipping the new army, and the khaki ran out; men paraded in make-shift dark-blue uniforms and black forage

Bottom left Comic postcard referring to the large numbers joining up in the first months of the war.

Bottom right An interesting postcard which shows that not everyone was impressed by the 'white feather' brigade who felt it was their duty to press men to join up.

caps. There were not enough barracks, so local men who volunteered were allowed to live at home. Many of the new volunteer units were entirely local. They were known as Pals battalions. Some were even more specific; the 1st Hull Battalion "the Commercials", was composed almost entirely of men drawn from commercial life. One correspondent to the London Mail that August called for *'a corps of gentlemen'* to be formed, composed of *'old public school boys and varsity men.'*

Kitchener raised the recruiting age to 35 and by the middle of September 1914, over 500,000 had volunteered. However, casualties in the British Expeditionary Force (B.E.F.), as the forces sent to France were called, were high; 57,000 by to the end of October - Kitchener called for a further 100,000 men.

The War Office posed 'Four Questions to the Women of England' including, *'Do you realise that the one word "Go" from you may send another man to fight for our King and Country?'* and *'When the War is over and your husband or your son is asked, "What did you do in the great War?" - is he*

"IV'E TRIED FOR THIRTY YEARS, AND CAN' GET ONE!" "LOR! AND HERE

"Why, aren't you in the Army?"
"Yus, and why aren't you in the Zoo?"

Both above Official badges given to men who worked in docks, munitions and other vital occupations to spare them from the attentions of those giving out white feathers.

Right Women munition workers wanted a badge, but there were those who argued against it. **Above** In 1916, they were finally given a badge of their own

to hang his head because you would not let him go? ... do your duty, send your men to-day to join our glorious Army.'

The middle and upper classes were asked: 'Have You a Butler, Groom, Chauffeur, Gardener or Gamekeeper serving you who at this moment should be serving your King and Country?

Have you a man serving at your table who should be serving a gun?

Have you a man digging your garden who should be digging trenches?

Have you a man driving your car who should be driving a transport wagon?

Have you a man preserving your game who should be helping to preserve your country?'

Members of the Active Service League, founded by Baroness Orczy, pledged 'to persuade every man I know to offer his services to the country, and I also pledge myself never to be seen in public with any man who, being in every way fit and free for service, has refused to respond to his country's call.'

Women handed out white feathers (a symbol of cowardice) to men and boys, regardless of their age, health, or suitability for military service. Lord Brockway claimed to have a collection which he spread out like a fan, while Lord Woolton later wrote how 'A pestilential body of women went round the country distributing white feathers to people in civilian clothes in entire ignorance of their circumstances.

THEY WANT TO TAKE MY BADGE AWAY !

'All the people engaged in the essential civil forces of the country were subjected to this form of persecution, which caused a great deal of unhappiness and it roused the fury of men home on leave - and often wounded - who were relaxing in civilian clothes and so attracted the attention of these unwanted and self-appointed recruiting persons.'

In response, many firms engaged on government work issued their male employees with badges declaring 'On Government Service' or similar; these were unofficial but were tolerated by the War Office. The Admiralty issued an 'On War Service 1914' badge to dockworkers. This was followed the following year by the 1915 Ministry of Munitions issue, and in 1916 a badge exclusively for female munitions workers. Women were not subjected to the white feather campaign, and there was some resistance to the idea of giving them badges. However the women argued that the badge was a symbol that they were 'doing their bit', and the government wisely accepted the argument.

The VTC

The government turned its attention to early anti-invasion groups. The idea of armed civilians roaming the countryside commanded by self-appointed leaders worried the authorities, and it was decided to take control of them. On 19 November 1914, 'The Central Association of Volunteer Training Corps' was recognised by the War Office. Only men who were not of an age to serve in the army or territorials, or were unable to do so for some genuine reason, could join this corps. No arms, ammunition, clothing, or money would be supplied from public funds, and no badges of rank allowed. However members could wear a uniform, as long as it was distinguishable from that of regular units. They bought their own uniforms, equipment and arms. To show they were official, when on duty, corps members could wear a red armband, bearing the royal monogram GR.

In March 1916, with the introduction of conscription, the VTC, was renamed the Volunteer Force, and was absorbed into the armed forces. A grey-green uniform became official and the red armlet was abolished.

Above Volunteer Training Corps lapel badge, worn off-duty.

Right The Volunteer Training Corps armband, bearing the Royal Monogram, to show they were an official body.

Above VTC and scout. Note the armband; most members of the VTC were men too old for the forces, like this gentleman.

The Spectator in April 1916 told its readers; *'What we may call the national interrogatory should run as follows: "Why are you not a soldier?" If the man answers: "Because I am over military age," the next question should be: "Why, then, are you not in a Volunteer battalion?"'*

National Registration

By the spring of 1915 enlistments were drying up. In May, in an effort to keep numbers up, the upper age limit was raised to 40. Originally men joining the army had to be at least 5ft 6in tall; now soldiers only had to be 5ft 3in tall, then in July the army

formed 'Bantam' battalions, composed of men between 5ft and 5ft 3in tall.

By now munitions were as important as recruitment to the services. Parliament ordered a register of every-one aged between 15 and 65. On 5 August an army of volunteers collected each person's name, date of birth and occupation. The names of men of military age, and their occupations, were passed to the recruiting authorities. To ensure co-operation, a pledge was given that the results would not be used for conscription, but to provide manpower statistics and to identify men who, in the national interest, should continue in their civilian roles.

Above National Registration card 1915. This buff one was a woman's card, while men's were khaki.

Right The inside of the Nation Registration card. Note the number (40) below his profession, There were 46 categories, some of which were starred (vital jobs). As recorded, Mr Dawson had attested under the Derby scheme.

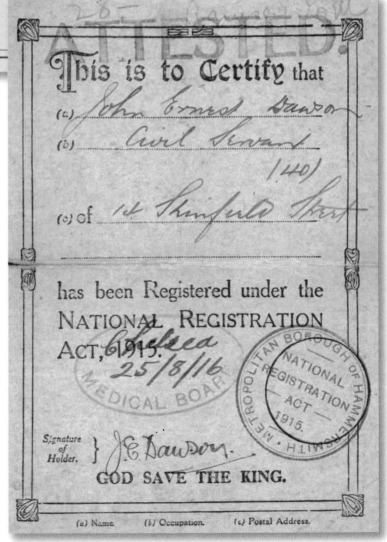

These were known as 'starred' jobs - men in essential occupations had a black star placed alongside their name and were often referred to as 'starred men'. At the time starred occupations were in munitions, branches of agriculture, coal-mining, railways, the merchant navy, and public utilities.

The census showed almost 5 million men of military age were not in the armed forces. Of those, 1.6 million were in starred jobs.

Right A Derby scheme armband. These were given to men who 'Attested' – promised to join up when called to do so.

Below A rather dapper gentleman wearing his Derby scheme armband.

The Derby Scheme

In September 1915 Lord Derby put forward a scheme to encourage volunteering without resorting to conscription; in October he was appointed Director-General of Recruiting, and in November his scheme was launched. Under it men of military age could take the oath of allegiance (attest), promising to join the army when called for. Those passed medically fit were divided into groups, indicating marital status, age, and usefulness to the war economy. Each would be called up in turn. 'Attesters' received khaki armlets bearing a red crown, and were allowed to continue their civilian jobs. The authorities promised that married men would not be called up before able-bodied single men, and no one under 19 would be called up.

On the final day for the scheme, Sunday 12 December, there was a last-minute rush at the recruiting stations, which stayed open till midnight. Worryingly for those who opposed conscription, over 650,000 unstarred single men had not attested. Consequently, at the end of the month the Cabinet approved the principle of conscription (which did not apply to Ireland).

Conscription

Early in 1916 Asquith introduced a bill bringing all single men between the ages of 18 and 41 into the Army; this soon became law. The Derby scheme was revived for one month from 10 January, after which conscription began, so that men might be spared the 'shame of compulsion'.

In May 1916, a second Military Service Act was introduced, covering all married men of military age. General exemptions included churchmen, those medically unfit or in vital jobs, those who supported relatives, and conscientious objectors. Local tribunals were set up to adjudicate on these claims. According to government instructions, the only married men in unstarred occupations likely to be released from military duties were the sole heads of businesses with a family of at least three depending on them.

A second area of appeal was on medical grounds. There were concerns about the number of men passed by the military doctors as medically fit for active service who included, in the records of one tribunal; *'...one applicant with severe valvular disease of the heart, and of another who not infrequently had three epileptic seizures in one week ... In September, 1917, we notice a case, by no means isolated, of a man rejected as unfit in 1915, passed for sedentary work in 1916, and now passed as fit. Of course, as soon as these facts appeared he was dismissed as unfit by the Tribunal.'*

Right Once called up you could appeal to the local tribunal – as the card indicates, a daunting task.

HOW I FELT BEFORE THE TRIBUNAL.

Below This postcard speaks for itself.

DUDLEY BUXTON

"Young man, where's your armlet?"

MILITARY SERVICE
COPY OF
VOUCHER ISSUED TO WREXHAM.

Montgomeryshire County Agricultural Executive Committee.

THIS IS TO CERTIFY THAT *[handwritten]*

employed by *[handwritten]*

was engaged on the 1st of June, 1917, as a whole-time agricultural worker, in the capacity of

that he is still so engaged, that his work is of national importance, and that this Committee are not prepared, for the time being, to consent to the man being posted for service with the Colours or being called up for medical examination or re-examination.

Signed *[handwritten signature]*

Secretary of the County Agricultural Executive Committee.

Date *[handwritten] June 13 — 1918*

P.T.O.

Above In 1918, local War Agricultural Committees, 'War Ags' as they were known, could issue certificates such as this, exempting vital land workers from conscription.

Conscientious objectors, or 'conchies' often had a hard time. Some, ordered into the army, took non-combatant roles; others refused and were sent to prison.

Many Derby recruits while awaiting their call-up, or during deferment, were directed by tribunals to attended drills with the local Volunteer Training Companies. This did not always go down well with the volunteers; in the case of the Dover VTC, for example; *'so faithful was this Company to the spirit of volunteering that it refused to admit men who were ordered to join the Volunteers by the Tribunals, as a condition of exemption from military service.'*

In April, 1918 at the time of the German spring offensive, the call-up age was extended to between 17 and 51. Far more contentiously, it also applied to Ireland and the Isle of Man, although it was never actually implemented in Ireland.

Above A mobile anti-aircraft gun. Note the naval uniforms; at the start of the war, the defence of the mainland fell to the navy.

Chapter 3

Enemy Attacks

Below A booklet containing photographs of the bomb and shell damage to the Hartlepools, Whitby and Scarborough.

The German Navy did not think it could beat the Royal Navy in an all-out confrontation. Instead it attempted to draw out small sections of the fleet by attacks on the British mainland. Such attacks would also play on invasion fears, diverting troops from France, and ships from the blockade of Germany. On 2 November, 1914, eight German cruisers arrived off Yarmouth, where

they shelled the wireless and naval air stations for fifteen minutes, achieving little, but demonstrating the potential for raiding.

Six weeks later, German battle-cruisers arrived off the mouth of the River Tees; three went to shell old Hartlepool and West Hartlepool; 100 people were killed, 300 wounded, and 600 houses damaged or destroyed. The other ships shelled Scarborough at close range; 12 people, including four children, were killed and over a hundred wounded.

Right Cannon Street anti-aircraft station, with the Monument to the Great Fire of London a poignant landmark in the distance.

Below A Zeppelin caught in the searchlight beams, note the anti-aircraft bursts around it.

There were further naval attacks throughout the war, usually by individual ships or U-Boats; in April, 1916, German ships attacked Lowestoft and Yarmouth, to support the Easter Uprising by Irish nationalists against British rule in Ireland.

By September 1914, rumours abounded of imminent raids by German airships. There were three types of German balloon; the Schütte-Lanz, Parseval and Zeppelin, but they became collectively known as Zeppelins, or more commonly, Zepps. Early Zeppelins were smaller than later versions, but they were still huge, from 500 to 600 feet long and 40 in diameter. They had a strong but light duralumin framework divided into several compartments; within each was a balloon, the whole encased within an outer envelope. These multiple balloons made it very difficult to shoot a Zeppelin down, as it could still fly even if several were knocked out.

Below London Special Constables wearing their newly-issued helmets to protect them from shrapnel in air raids (1917).

In January 1915 the Kaiser gave permission for airship raids on Britain, restricted to military establishments. The City of London was specifically not to be bombed.

The Admiralty were responsible for the aerial protection of mainland Britain, providing aircraft, in the form of the Royal Naval Air Service, for the defence of ports, and anti-aircraft guns for large cities. The guns defending ports and other vulnerable points were the responsibility of the army. Planes were sent up to assess the visibility of London by night and restricted lighting was introduced in October. Police in a sixty-mile radius of London warned the capital of the approach of hostile aircraft. Special Constables, who would later form the Observer Corps,

Above China model (front and back) of a bomb dropped by a zeppelin on Bury St Edmunds in April 1915. Such small china knick-knacks were very popular holiday souvenirs.

kept watch. Towards the end of 1914 the London anti-aircraft defences formed a circle with a six-mile radius from Charing Cross. It was made up of 12 guns, and 12 searchlights, the latter manned by volunteers including Special Constables.

On 19 January, 1915, three Zeppelins began the assault. One had to turn back but the others reached Norfolk. One flew over Yarmouth, dropping nine bombs, which killed two and injured three. The other circled north-eastern Norfolk, dropping bombs randomly until King's Lynn, where it unloaded seven high explosive bombs and the last of its incendiaries, leaving two dead and 13 injured.

British casualties were small compared to the cost and risk of the operation to the Germans, yet the morale effects on British civilians were out of all proportion to the casualties. Nerviness, 'Zeppitus' as it was called, spread. Steel nets were suspended over Buckingham Palace, the War Office, and other distinguished buildings, to deflect bombs, and the lake in St James's Park was drained so as not to serve as a direction-marker. The area covered by police observers was extended to East Anglia, Northamptonshire, Oxfordshire, Hampshire, and the Isle of Wight.

One early idea was to recruit blind people. Their ability to hear distant engines was deemed to be greater than that of sighted people. In south-east England, they formed a listening service which fed range and altitude to the defences. In early experiments, a blind man was fitted with a stethoscope to intensify hearing and a pole was attached to his head. He would turn in the direction of the raider and indicate the bearing. Listening posts consisting of stethoscopes attached to wide-mouthed, rotatable 'trumpets' were eventually worked with some success by sighted people.

The next few raids were not, as the nervous feared, by dozens of Zepps bringing hundreds of deaths. Raids by single Zepps, or by two or three in concert were the norm, usually on eastern towns and cities. They crept ever nearer to the capital. In February there were small attacks by aeroplanes over southern and eastern coastal towns, but it was not until mid-April that the 'Zepps' returned, raiding Tyneside, the east coast and East Anglia. On 31 May Greater London was attacked for the first time. A single Zeppelin dropped bombs, mainly on the East End, killing seven people and injuring thirty-five.

The German Chiefs of Staff pressed the Kaiser; it would, they argued, be a mistake to spare the City of London. He finally gave permission for raids on the city in July 1915. The only restriction was that buildings of historic interest such as St Paul's and

Above German postcard showing 'the angst of Londoners over the Zeppelins', in reality such panic was rare.

Westminster Abbey were not to be damaged, though accurate bombing was impossible.

The shock of the new wore off, and by October the London Opinion newspaper reported that *'the dreadful truth is that London regards a Zeppelin very much as an elephant regards a flea.'* One reason for this was, as one German commander reported; *"we could take with us only three one-hundredweight high-explosive and about twenty incendiary bombs, small things weighing about 7 lb each"* Later Super-Zeppelins, would carry far heavier loads.

Despite their size, Zeppelins seemed impossible to shoot down. Flying as they did at night, they were almost unopposed by British planes. Night-flying had been thought impossible; now it proved possible, but very dangerous – many pilots were killed on take-off or landing. If you did spot a Zeppelin, you had to climb to reach them (during which time they would usually escape).

On the night of 2 September 1916, Lieutenant William Leefe Robinson, flying a B.E.2c night fighter, sighted a Schütte-Lanz over Cuffley in Hertfordshire. The airship was one of 16 on a mass raid. Attacking from below, he raked the airship with machine-gun fire; it burst into flames and crashed in a field at Cuffley, killing the crew. By now Zepp-watching – going out into the street to watch the airships – was rife. Londoners, as they

THE
FINEST SIGHT
I EVER SAW!

IT DIDN'T LAST A VERY LONG TIME
SO IT WON'T TAKE LONG TO TELL —
'TWAS WHEN I SAW, IN THE HEAVENS SUBLIME,
THE GERMANS GOING TO *√½½*

saw the airship descend in flames, cheered and sang the national anthem, one even played the bagpipes. The propaganda value was enormous to the British; the Zeppelins could be beaten.

Robinson was awarded the Victoria Cross. His victory owed much to developments in technology; as they could rarely reach the same height as a balloon, aircraft were now fitted with upward–firing guns; and rather than normal bullets, they carried alternate explosive and incendiary bullets, the first to blow a hole in the airship, the second to ignite the resulting mixture of escaping gas and air. With the success of theses anti-Zeppelin measures, the winter of 1916-1917 saw a lull in the aerial assault. Lighting restrictions were, as a result, eased.

Above Postcard celebrating the shooting down of the first Zeppelin over Britain in September 1916.

Right A downed Gotha draws great crowds at a National Savings fund-raising event.

In May 1917 the Germans began assaults with Gothas, twin-engined aircraft, which soon restored the balance in the Germans' favour. In a daylight attack on London on 13 June, fourteen Gothas dropped 118 high explosive and incendiary bombs on the City and the East End of London. This caused the greatest casualties of any attack of the war, with 162 killed and 426 injured.

Above Zepp watching. After the initial panic, many people found the Zeppelins, the searchlights and the anti-aircraft guns to be a great free show.

A balloon apron was added to the system of searchlights, anti-aircraft guns and sound-detecting stations. This apron was a series of slender steel wires suspended from cross cables attached to the mooring cables of balloons flying at a height of 8,000 feet. The intention was that raiding aircraft would collide with the wires and be bought down.

In late summer 1917, the Germans changed tactics again; daylight raids gave way to aeroplane attacks by moonlight. In December warnings were introduced throughout London, but only during daytime; only in March 1918 was the use of maroons at any hour of the day or night authorized.

Daylight attacks that summer caused large crowds to seek shelter in the London Underground; the moonlight attacks of September had caused panic among sections of the East End. 'Trekking' into the safer western districts became a common practice, while police stations were allowed to be used as shelters. Other public buildings followed suit, and an order of October 1917 allowed other premises to be requisitioned. Outside London, despite criticism, local authorities were responsible for providing shelters

The attack on London on Whit Sunday, 19 May, 1918, was the last serious raid on Britain. There had been 103 bombing raids (51 by airships and 52 by aeroplanes); about 300 tons of bombs were dropped causing 4,820 casualties, including 1,413 dead. London bore a large share of the attacks. About one-quarter of the the bombs dropped of bombs dropped in the UK fell on the Metropolitan Police District, causing 670 deaths and injury to 1,960.

Chapter 4

War Work

The demands of war meant that 'War factories' sprang up everywhere. Large factories and small workshops switched to making war weapons such as cartridge cases, buckles, belts, etc. New premises opened up and existing ones expanded, It was evident that output had to increase and large numbers of workers were needed. During the free-for-all rush for volunteers for the forces, many munitions workers had enlisted. Trade unions had agreed to give up strikes 'for the duration', and also to the idea of dilution, replacing skilled workers with unskilled men and women. Soon, unskilled men and women were taken on in large numbers. There were protests against women coming into workplaces, but the prevailing view was that such rules needed to be suspended for the war.

The rush to set up a huge munitions industry created problems -- disorganisation, low production and a high proportion of faulty products not least. The government was attacked over shortages of shells at the front. In March 1915 Lloyd George voiced his concern at "the grave situation" in armament factories. In response, in mid-April, a committee was appointed under his chairmanship. Many felt that the situation reflected the government's failure to realize the gravity of the situation; Asquith was forced to accept calls for a coalition government, which was formed on 25 May. In mid-June the Ministry of Munitions was created, with Lloyd George as Minister.

New, giant factories had to be built before the mass entry of women into munitions could take place. This was not soon enough for Mrs Pankhurst who, in July, led 30,000 women through London, accompanied by 90 bands, demanding war work. Their protest was funded in part by a grant from Lloyd George. He agreed with her that, at that time, Britain had only 50,000 women in munitions as against Germany's 500,000. A little under a year later, in May 1916, he reported that there were by then 300,000 women working in the filling factories, engineering works and shipyards. To accomplish this, the Ministry of Munitions started a large number of training centres

IT'LL TAKE TWO WOMEN TO FILL MY PLACE.

Above Up and down the country, women were filling men's places in a wide range of jobs.

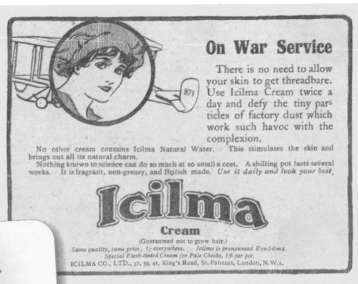

On War Service

There is no need to allow your skin to get threadbare. Use Icilma Cream twice a day and defy the tiny particles of factory dust which work such havoc with the complexion.

No other cream contains Icilma Natural Water. This stimulates the skin and brings out all its natural charm.
Nothing known to science can do so much at so small a cost. A shilling pot lasts several weeks. It is fragrant, non-greasy, and British made. Use it daily and look your best.

Icilma
Cream
(Guaranteed not to grow hair.)

Same quality, same price, 1/- everywhere. Icilma is pronounced Eye-Silma.
Special Flesh-tinted Cream for Pale Cheeks, 1/6 per pot.
ICILMA CO., LTD., 37, 39, 41, King's Road, St. Pancras, London, N.W.1.

Right Munitions work could be very hard on the hands and faces of the women workers.

Above Typical group of 'munitionettes', as female munitions workers were called.

around the country. In the better establishments, women's health was looked after. Ventilation was installed, and those who worked with dangerous materials were supplied with protective clothing; for example, those working with acids wore clogs instead of ordinary shoes. Women working became not only acceptable, but patriotic. Walter Long, a Conservative, said *'There are still places where women believe their place is the home; that idea must be met and combatted.'*

The demand for munitions meant factories worked round the clock; this inevitably led to accidents. The worst was on 19 January 1917, when the TNT factory at Silvertown, East London, blew up. 73 people, including thirteen women and seventeen children were killed. The concussion shook every house in Croydon, more than twelve miles away.

Workers, now predominantly women, might blow their fingers off in the shell-filling factories where their faces turned bright yellow, and their hair fell out. So hideous were the 'Canaries', as they were dubbed, that they were turned away from eating-places. To guard against toxic jaundice from TNT they were supposed to cover their faces with grease and even wear respirators, but the precautions were nearly as unpleasant as the complaint. Jaundice could be fatal; 52 women died of it in 1916 and 42 in 1917. Another dangerous job was filling poison gas shells; in 1918 1,300 women were gassed to

Below A 'shift' was a popular name for a dress, so working in a night shift also meant working in a nightdress!

Below A 'shift' was a popular name for a dress, so working in a night shift also meant working in a nightdress!

Above Miss Rhoda Broderick, a patrol leader of the Croydon Voluntary Women Patrols, Such patrols were set up in many places.

varying extents in one factory producing mustard-gas shells near Henbury. During the war and after, many more died of cancers and other long-term conditions caused by exposure to the chemicals they worked with.

Men and women in munitions might be taken before tribunals for disciplinary offences. In Glasgow four girls who refused to wear trousers appealed against dismissal, but the sheriff ruled that male attire was a condition of employment.

Because of the dangers, munitions work was well paid; in 1916 it was said that piano dealers had never been so prosperous; others commented on the rage for furs and fancy nightgowns. That summer, newspapers were outraged at the high prices paid by war workers for furnished holiday apartments. There were also concerns about young workers, who could start work at age of twelve. For instance, at Woolwich Arsenal, one of the largest factories, boys worked a twelve-hour day. 'Pearson's Weekly' pointed out that 35% of working boys were engaged on war work, and that 35% of working girls were either doing war work or work done by boys before the war.

In July 1914, 24% of the workforce were women; by the end of April 1918, this had increased to 37%. Of these, one-and-a-half million had directly replaced men.

From September 1916 the Ministry of Munitions stationed policewomen in munitions factories. They examined passes, searched for contraband, and travelled on workmen's trains to keep order.

While men not in uniform were often treated with scorn, those in uniform could be treated with what Pearson's Magazine called *'indiscriminate khaki hero-worship.'* To this end, many women and girls would hang around training camps; military authorities complained that they were a nuisance. In London, early in the war, the police asked the National Union of Women Workers to set up Voluntary Women Patrols (VWPs) to go out among the women and girls visiting London's army camps, parks, recruiting stations and railway terminals. Within a few months more than 500 women had enrolled in the patrols, and the idea spread throughout the country.

The VWPs worked in pairs, patrolling for two hours in the evening. They wore a uniform of a heavy blue coat and skirt, black hat, and an armlet. Their stated aim was to *'prevent the ignorant from falling'*. They intervened when they saw girls speaking to men on duty, shone torches on couples sitting next to each other in cinemas and on public benches, and would occupy vacant seats next to couples in public places. They

Above left A post-woman. Women replaced men in jobs as diverse as chauffeurs, railway porters, delivering coal, and horse-breaking.

Above right On the right, a 'clippie', as female bus conductors were called; the short hemline and high leather boots date this from 1916 or 1917.

patrolled cinemas, parks, the underground and other stations, telling women they deemed to be at risk to leave the area and putting women in touch with local societies, clubs, or classes. The patrols also met soldiers' leave trains. They were not universally welcome. In 1915, an angry correspondent wrote to the East Grinstead Observer, 'It is about time something was done about ancient spinsters following soldiers about with their flashlights. I have seen a great deal of the soldiers … and I consider that they have been unfairly treated. Walking in the roads and fields accompanied by friends is no crime. What would these spinsters think if soldiers flashed a light upon them in their gardens or darkened drawing rooms?'

Few women worked in banks pre-war, but during the war, their numbers rapidly increased until, in 1918, they outnumbered men by five to one. In the Post Office, in Portsmouth for example, 447 men were employed before the war. Of these, 266 were released for military service and were replaced by 261 women, not only in the post offices, but as post-women, and in the telegraph department. In public transport women also replaced men in large numbers. On the trains, they were lift operators, ticket collectors, porters, ticket inspectors, and booking-office clerks. On buses and trams, 'clippies', as female conductors were called, became the norm. By the end of the war there were few areas of work where women were not represented. They drove carts delivering all manner of goods, cleaned windows, and swept chimneys. Their job titles were different to those of the men who had done the work pre-war – now the work was done by carterettes, conductresses and, in garages, 'petrol nymphs'.

Agriculture

During the first year of the war, the government generally left agricultural policy to the individual farmer, although the Department of Agriculture banned the slaughter of calves, in-calf cows and pregnant sows, to safeguard breeding stocks.

Below Indiscriminate recruiting meant that many vital industries, including farming, were left short of workers.

Farmers were doing well; by December 1914 the price of wheat had gone up by 25%, and by May 1915, 80%, and sheep prices were 40% up by June. However, imports of feedstuffs, and fertilisers were badly hit.

" Why aren't you at the Front, my man ? "
" 'Cos there aint no milk that end, Miss !! "

The rush to the recruiting offices resulted in the loss of 15% of agricultural labourers by January 1915, mainly the youngest and fittest. Suggested solutions to the growing labour-shortage included more soldier-labour, the employment of more women; and that leave should be given to schoolchildren over thirteen for such seasonal work as potato planting and gathering; in many rural districts leave was already given between September and December for boys from the age of eleven to help with the harvest.

The advent of conscription made the agricultural labour shortage acute; by the end of that May 1916, one-third of agricultural workers had left the land. That month, Lloyd George said that in his young days a far larger proportion of women had been engaged in agricultural work, and, if needs demanded, they could still look after the farms to let the men fight. Faced with disaster, the Government authorized the temporary release of 12,000 to 15,000 soldiers to assist in the harvest, and more women began to work on the land. Consequently, that year's wheat crop was average; unfortunately the potato crop was 25% down on normal years.

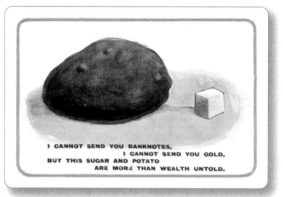

I CANNOT SEND YOU BANKNOTES,
I CANNOT SEND YOU GOLD,
BUT THIS SUGAR AND POTATO
ARE MORE THAN WEALTH UNTOLD.

Above By 1915, shortages of basic food items, such as potatoes and sugar, were driving up prices.

In the summer of 1915 the Women's Farm and Garden Union realised the problems of putting untrained women to work on the land. That autumn they set up 'training farms', where women went on six-month courses to become members of the Women's National Land Service Corps.

Each County or County Division was asked to appoint a 'County Agricultural Executive Committee', to act as local agents of the Board of Agriculture. Farmers were considered the best judges of what could be achieved locally, and which unused land was most suitable for ploughing-up. During 1918, they were also given the responsibility of vetting farm worker recruits for the Army.

The first Cultivation of Lands Order, giving the County Executive Committees wide-ranging powers, came into force on January 1917. If a committee felt grassland could be better used for arable crops, they could serve notice requiring it to be broken up, or plough it up themselves. There was no appeal and failure to comply could lead to a fine or imprisonment. In April the Board of Agriculture took measures to break up grassland and bring it under tillage. Paddocks, parklands and ornamental gardens were cultivated, even Kew Gardens. Under the board's direction, the area under hops was reduced by half; that under mustard by two-thirds, and the land freed for food crops. In Scotland before the war, many hill farms had been cleared and the land converted to 'deer forests'. Now the Scottish Board of Agriculture pressed owners to graze sheep and cattle on the

Top Members of the Timber Corps of the WLA, with the tools of their trade.

Right Traunee members of the Woman's Land Army

forestland during the summer. In March the Food Controller announced that pheasants, hares and rabbits could be shot all the year round. At the same time, artificial feeding of deer and pheasants was prohibited, so that foodstuffs should not be wasted.

By July 1917, 28% of farm workers were in the Army. From that date, however, a regular weekly quota of agricultural labourers were released. This and other schemes added 70,000 to 80,000 workers to the land. Such new land and fresh labour, combined with an unusually good harvest secured an additional three weeks' supply of homegrown wheat.

Demand for women trained by the National Land Service Corps became too great for a small voluntary association, and the Women's Land Army was formed in February 1917. It was divided into three sections; agricultural, forage, or timber cutting. Land Girls, as they became known, were recruited for six months or a year, and sent for training. Upon successfully passing an efficiency test, they would be given full-time employment at a minimum wage of £1 a week. They found, or were found, work anywhere in the UK, living on the farms, in local billets, or in WLA hostels.

Below A women's Land Army armlet awarded after 30 days work on the land; this one has service stripes, one for every six months' land work.

Under the Hague Convention prisoners of war, except officers, could be used for work. By the autumn of 1917, 70,000 German prisoners were employed in harvesting, digging potatoes and threshing. After the previous year's poor potato harvest, farmers were told to grow potatoes as well as oats in greater quantities, Lloyd George said he hoped to provide 30,000 unskilled labourers, 15,000 horses and 8,000 tractors by the middle of March.

Right A trainee member (with armband) leads a horse from its stable. The WLA carried out agricultural jobs including field work, working with animals, driving tractors, and many other tasks.

There was a renewed call for men for the army early in 1918; young male land-workers, previously exempt, were called up. The potato harvest was at hand, and unless there was to be another shortage farmers had to be provided with labour. An appeal was made to schoolboys to give up part of their holidays to help; in late April 'The Scout' told its readers; *'Scouts! Once more there is a call to you from your country. It is to back up our splendid fellows at the Front'.*

In spite of this, the shortage of labour became acute. In June, a further 22,000 experienced farm workers were called up; that year the Board supplied 72,000 soldiers, 30,000 POWs, 4,000 War Agricultural Volunteers, and 15,000 public school-boys -- a total of 122,000 men. The Women's Division provided 300,000 part-time workers, and 16,000 Land Girls. All this meant

Right Working with a horse-drawn plough.

that farming not only continued, but expanded. In England and Wales an additional 290,000 acres were brought under the plough.

In July a good corn harvest was expected; in the south of England, the crops were gathered in, but in the north, the weather broke before the harvest. Even this could not outweigh an overall abundant crop. But improved corn and potato harvests came at some cost; livestock production was down, but overall the net gain in food was huge. By 1919, the campaign for increased production had added almost 3 million acres to the area cultivated in the UK. Late that year the Women's Land Army was disbanded; over 260,000 women had worked on the land during the war, 23,000 of them in the WLA.Many felt that women's efforts during the war meant that they could not be denied the vote, but for the majority, this continued to be the case. The Representation of the People Act in February 1918 gave all men over the age of 21 the vote. Women over 30 could vote if they were registered property owners or married to a man who was, or if they were graduates in a university town. About 8 million women qualified. Portsmouth was the first town in which the new electorate voted and in November 1918, Kate Edmonds was elected to the city council by a majority of over 600 votes.

OUT FOR VICTORY.

THE FARM GIRL.
Who is doing her bit to feed us all.

Below Good Service badge awarded for six months entirely satisfactory work and conduct.

Chapter 5

Food

In 1914 Britain imported a third of the food it consumed, including all its sugar, three-quarters of its wheat, butter, and margarine, and a quarter of beef and mutton. This left it vulnerable to attacks on shipping. Most of Germany's fleet was tied up by the Royal Navy's blockade, so it tried to use submarines. Ships entering this German Blockade could be attacked without warning. Many were sunk, including, in May 1915, the liner Lusitania, with the loss of 1200 lives, 120 of whom were US citizens. Such losses threatened to bring the USA into the war, and Germany was forced to reverse the policy. In 1917 the German attacks began again, in the hope that Britain would give in before American patience snapped.

The British Government's policy was one of laissez-faire - shortages would be reflected by price rises, which would dampen demand. In the first two years of the war, this policy led to many items doubling in price. The Government did little; it told people to eat less of the shortage items, and asked the rich to eat only luxury items, thus leaving the basics for the poor.

In January 1917, in response to a growing out-cry about shortages and price rises, the Ministry of Food was created under a 'Food Controller', Lord Devonport. Local Food Committees were set up to oversee the supply and distribution of food in their area. People were urged to 'Eat Less Bread' -- one way being to substi-tute an extra potato for bread with a meal. The Government introduced a standard wholemeal loaf, called G.R. (Government Regulation) bread, pop-ularly known as 'war bread.'.

In February the Government ordered that wheat flour be mixed with rice, barley, maize, and other cereals. At the same time currant, sultana, and milk breads, and the use of sugar in bread, were banned. By mid-November the use of 12½% potatoes in bread was permitted, and in April 1918, local food committees were allowed to make the use of pota-toes in bread compulsory.

All sugar was imported, so the Ministry encouraged people to do without, especially sweets or pastries which were seen as self-indulgent and unpatriotic. In 1916, confectionery manufactur-ers were ordered to cut production to just 25% of that of 1915, and the commercial use of sugar as a dusting or icing on cakes was banned. Sugar was also not to be used in chocolates, followed a year later by a ban on the use of milk.

The Ministry of Food appealed to people to follow a scheme of voluntary rationing of 4 lbs bread, 2½ lbs meat, and ¾ lb sugar per person per week and came with a warn-ing that if this failed, compulsion must follow.

Early in 1917 there was a shortage of potatoes; in April the Ministry announced everyone should have five potato-less days a week, the exceptions being Wednesdays and Fridays.

Above The liner Lusitania was sunk by a U-Boat in May 1915, with over 1,000 deaths. In Germany a medal was made which was sold to the public. In Britain the sinking caused outrage and riots; German shops were looted, and British copies of the medal, such as this, were sold.

Opposite page Poster for the League of National Safety, a group set up by the Ministry of Food to encourage people to eat less.

About the only thing that's come down since the war!

JOIN THE
LEAGUE of NATIONAL SAFETY

FOOD ECONOMY
NATIONAL
SAFETY

"I risked my life

"to bring you Food. Use it
"carefully—live on Voluntary
"Rations and Win the War."

Write to The Ministry of Food, GROSVENOR HOUSE, W.1

MINISTRY OF FOOD   CLARKE & SHERWELL, LTD., PRINTERS, LONDON

Right The Win the War Cookery Book, a recipe book published by the Food Economy Campaign, encouraging the use of non-shortage ingredients.

THE **2D**

WIN-THE-WAR COOKERY BOOK

EAT ONE POUND LESS BREAD PER WEEK THAN YOU ARE EATING NOW

PUBLISHED FOR THE FOOD ECONOMY CAMPAIGN

WITH THE APPROVAL OF THE MINISTRY OF FOOD

YES- COMPLETE VICTORY IF YOU EAT LESS BREAD

Below A Grocer's potato card from 1917. Many grocer's served shortage items only to regular customers.

POTATO TICKET
Issued by DALLAWAYS
during Potato Famine.

GREAT WAR, 1917.

This ticket is issued to regular buyers at Dallaways living in Smethwick with the object of preventing persons from outlying districts obtaining the supply that Mr. Dallaway intends for his own customers.

This ticket does not guarantee a supply, but only means that the holder can purchase when a supply is on sale.

If this ticket is used twice in one day it will be cancelled.
You are requested to inform against persons misusing.

I, the undersigned, am a regular buyer at Dallaways, and reside in Smethwick.

Name..

Address ....

On other days shops could not sell potatoes and the public was encouraged to find alternatives, such as rice. The huge increase in allotments helped end the crisis, and in July potato-less days were cancelled.

In April 1917 under the Food Hoarding Order any stock of food which *'exceeds the quantity required for ordinary use and consumption in his household or establishment'* was banned. The problem was that it did not actually spell out what was regarded as an acceptable amount. Fines, and the stores that prompted prosecutions, could be huge; one man from Walsall was found to have in his cellars 424 lb. of tea, 311 lb. of bacon and ham, 175 lb. of flour, 133 lb. of biscuits, 127 lb. of sugar, 9 sacks of potatoes, 455 tins of meat, fish, fruit and condensed milk, 700

Right Importing, as we did, all our sugar, left the country short of sugar, which became the first item of food to be regulated.

Butter is dear

—too dear for many purses, so try 'Pheasant.'

'Pheasant'has always the same appetising freshness, the distinctively delicate flavour, the purity of faultless ingredients.

Ask your Grocer for it.

PHEASANT MARGARINE

The Superior Brand of Margarine.

PER LB. **1'-** PER LB.

Pheasant Margarine is sold in ½lb. packages, with the red, white and blue riband and the Pheasant Seal.

Above Like other foods, the price of butter soared throughout the war, creating real problems for the poorest sections of the population.

lb. of other foodstuffs, 9 gallons of vinegar, 10 dozen bottles of ale, 166 bottles of wine, and 28 of spirits. He was sentenced to six months' imprisonment, and fined £50, with costs.

In May, the King issued a proclamation urging his subjects to practice economy, especially in grain; it was read in churches of every denomination for the next four Sundays. Wasting food became an offence. Within days, a woman from Bromley was fined £5 for wasting 4lb. of bread found in her dustbin, and another woman was fined £5 for burning a quantity of stale bread on her lawn, in spite of her solicitor's plea that she had *'acted under provocation on the part of her husband.'*

Maximum prices for butter were fixed that August, and for margarine in November. Butter became scarce, so margarine was widely used instead, and the Ministry of Food recommended cocoa butter for cooking.

In September 1917, the ministry set up the Food Economy Department; speakers gave lectures on preparing, cooking, and preserving food. They visited schools, showing children how to *'eat carefully'* and waste nothing. Conferences presented papers and demonstrations on economical methods

Below right Ministry of Food Postcard from April 1917. The reverse reads; 'The Food Controller would be glad if you would show this card in your window or any other conspicuous place in order to help the scheme of Voluntary Rationing.'

of cooking, for the mistresses of large households and their cooks. Leaflets advised on wartime recipes, hay-box cookery, voluntary rations and other topics, and a handbook was produced.

The League of National Safety was part of the food economy campaign. Nearly 4 million members wore the league's Anchor Badge, having pledged to follow voluntary rationing. There was also a Junior League for children under 16 who collected waste, especially in rural districts.

IN HONOUR BOUND
WE ADOPT
THE NATIONAL SCALE
OF
VOLUNTARY RATIONS

Below Shortages led to ever increasing food queues, as this play on the popular song-title of the period depicts

THERE'S A LONG LONG TRAIL AWINDING.

POTATOES TO-DAY

In mid-November a new scale of voluntary rationing was issued, giving different amounts of bread for men, women and heavy workers. It also included cereals (¾ lb each), butter, margarine and lard, (total 10 oz). Milk and cheese were reserved for persons for whom they were essential, while more use would be made of fresh vegetables and fruit -- in particular, potatoes.

In December 1917 Lord Rhondda stated that: *'There is no problem which has given me and my staff so much anxiety as that of the queues. ...It is mainly a question of distribution.'* That month local food committees were given powers to bring in local rationing schemes to prevent food queues. This meant banning retailers from

Above The League of National safety was set up to encourage people to follow voluntary rationing. Those joining received a membership card, and the league's anchor badge.

Now! don't you know this is our meatless day

THE END OF A PERFECT DAY.

Above left and below

Meat was another shortage foodstuff, leading, at the beginning of 1918, to the introduction of 'Meatless Days'.

with vegetables helps to economise meat.

Here is another suggestion for an OXO and vegetable dish which is particularly appropriate to the present time.

AN OXO VEGETABLE PIE
(enough for four persons).

selling specified goods, except to customers registered with them. It was made clear that no-one could register at more than one shop. Pontypool was the first town to adopt such a scheme. It began on 17 December and covered butter, tea, bacon, margarine, cheese, lard, and jam; Birmingham soon followed. However, it was only when national rationing arrived that the problem of queues would be fully resolved; in London, one month after the national scheme began, queues had dropped by at least 95%.

In January 1918 Sir Edward Coates, M.P., said: "*Weigh yourself now and again three months hence, and if you have lost half a stone or so you will know you are a good patriot.*"

Early in 1918, no meat, cooked or uncooked, could be sold on two specified 'meatless days' a week. Some people called for non-working dogs to be put down, others for compulsory rationing. The Ministry of Food declared an amnesty for people who were unsure whether their stores were within acceptable limits. For a week in February, 'Conscience week', people could send to the local food office any food they thought was in excess of 'ordinary requirements.' This was then sold to the 'deserving poor', with the owner receiving half the proceeds.

Opposite page, top left
A depiction of a popular song title. Look at the huge grin and the tiny parcels.

Left Child's ration card from the London and Home Counties scheme of early 1918.

Below the King's meat card, from the same scheme, reproduced to demonstrate that everyone got the same.

(21593). Wt. 22098/351. 320,000. 3/18. M⁰C. & Co., Ltd. (E. 2473).

CHILD'S FOOD CARD. ■■■ D. 5. S.W.

South Western Division.

Holder's Name _Kathleen M. Rutter_

Address _33. St Leonard's Avenue_ EXETER.

CUSTOMER'S PART.

| A. BUTTER AND MARGARINE | X | X | X | X | 5 | 6 | 7 | 8 | 9 | 10 |
| | 11 | 12 | 13 | 14 | 15 | 16 | 17 | 18 | 19 | 20 |

| B, | X | X | X | X | 5 | 6 | 7 | 8 | 9 | 10 |
| | 11 | 12 | 13 | 14 | 15 | 16 | 17 | 18 | 19 | 20 |

| C, | X | X | X | X | 5 | 6 | 7 | 8 | 9 | 10 |
| | 11 | 12 | 13 | 14 | 15 | 16 | 17 | 18 | 19 | 20 |

| D, | X | X | X | X | 5 | 6 | 7 | 8 | 9 | 10 |
| | 11 | 12 | 13 | 14 | 15 | 16 | 17 | 18 | 19 | 20 |

D. _Rutter_

Shopkeeper's Name : _Kathleen Marion Rutter_

Address : _33 St Leonards Avenue Exeter_

's Name :

LONDON AND HOME COUNTIES. Meat Card D 7.

(See Instructions overleaf.)

Butcher's Names:- { HALL AND SON. } { DURING FEBRUARY. }
{ GASLIN AND CO. } { MARCH. }
{ J. RATCLIFF. } { APRIL. }
Butcher's Address { W. ALLEN AND CO. } { MAY. }

9	9	9	9	10	10	10	10
11	11	11	11	12	12	12	12
13	13	13	13	14	14	14	14
20	20	MEAT CARD [L. and H C.]			15	16	
20	20	Office of Issue			15	16	
		A. Holder's Name:—					
		His Majesty The King					
19	19	Address:—			16	16	
		Buckingham Palace					
19	19	_S.W._			16	16	
		B. Holder's Signature:—					
		George R.I.					
18	18	C. Butcher's Name and Address:—			17	17	
18	18				17	17	
		IF FOUND, DROP IN A PILLAR BOX.					
8	8	8	8	7	7	7	7
6	6	6	6	5	5	5	5
4	4	4	4	3	3	3	3
2	2	2	2	1	1	1	1

The King's Meat Card.

There was a widespread feeling that sacrifices should be equally shared; calls for national rationing grew ever more strident. In February a unified scheme was introduced in London and the Home Counties. Individuals registered with a butcher and a grocer, and were issued with a meat card and a butter and margarine card, on which were printed numbered coupons. Butter and margarine were rationed by weight; ¼ lb a week in total for everyone. Later this was changed to 1oz. of butter and 4oz. of margarine. Meat was rationed by value; adults could buy 1s. 8d. worth of meat weekly, and children half that.

On the whole the scheme worked well and in April it was introduced nation-wide. The cards were replaced by ration books containing sixteen weeks' worth of coupons for sugar, fats, butcher's meat, and bacon. Each coupon was numbered and

IF FOUND, RETURN TO ANY FOOD OFFICE.

MINISTRY OF FOOD.
CHILD'S RATION BOOK (A).

INSTRUCTIONS.

Read carefully these instructions and the leaflet which will be sent you with this Book.

1. The parent or guardian of the child named on the reference leaf as the holder of this ration book must sign his own name and write the child's name and address in the space below, and write the child's name and address, and the serial number (printed upside down on the back cover) in the space provided to the left of each page of coupons.

Food Office of Issue .... EXETER .... Date .... 21 OCT 1918

Signature of Child's Parent or Guardian .... *C. A. Rutter*

Name of Child .... *Evelyn Rutter*

Address .... *33 St Leonards Ave Exeter*

2. For convenience of writing at the Food Office the Reference Leaf has been put opposite the back cover, and has purposely been printed upside down. It should be carefully examined. If there is any mistake in the entries on the Reference Leaf, the Food Office should be asked to correct it.

3. The book must be registered at once by the child's parent or guardian, who must take the book to the retailers with whom the child was previously registered for butcher's meat, bacon, butter and margarine, sugar and tea respectively, or, if the child has not previously held a book, to any retailers chosen. These retailers must write their names and the addresses of their shops in the proper space on the back of the cover. The books of children staying in hotels, boarding houses, hostels, schools and similar establishments should not be registered until they leave the establishment.

4. The ration book may be used only by or on behalf of the holder, to buy rationed food for him, or members of the same household, or guests sharing common meals. It may not be used to buy rationed food for any other persons.

[Continued on next page.

IF FOUND, RETURN TO ANY FOOD OFFICE.

MINISTRY OF FOOD.
NATIONAL RATION BOOK (B).

INSTRUCTIONS.

Read carefully these instructions and the leaflet which will be sent you with this Book.

1. The person named on the reference leaf as the holder of this ration book must write his name and address in the space below, and must write his name and address, and the serial number (printed upside down on the back cover), in the space provided to the left of each page of coupons.

Food Office of Issue .... EXETER .... Date .... 21 OCT 1918

Signature of Holder .... *Catherine Rutter*

Address .... *33 St Leonards Ave Exeter*

2. For convenience of writing at the Food Office the Reference Leaf has been put opposite the back cover, and has purposely been printed upside down. It should be carefully examined. If there is any mistake in the entries on the Reference Leaf, the Food Office should be asked to correct it.

3. The holder must register this book at once by getting his retailers for butcher's meat, bacon, butter and margarine, sugar and tea respectively, to write their names and the addresses of their shops in the proper space on the back of the cover. Persons staying in hotels, boarding houses, hostels, schools, and similar establishments should not register their books until they leave the establishment.

4. The ration book may be used only by or on behalf of the holder, to buy rationed food for him, or members of the same household, or guests sharing common meals. It may not be used to buy rationed food for any other persons.

N. 2 (Nov.)   *[Continued on next page.*

IF FOUND, RETURN TO ANY FOOD OFFICE.

MINISTRY OF FO
SUPPLEMENTA

1. The person named as the holder (page 1) (Magenta) must sign his name spaces provided for them on the Referen cover and the Serial Number appearing

2. The Book must be registered a sign his name and enter his address and take the book to the bacon retaile proper space (numbered 1) on the inside detach and keep the counterfoil.

3. A person who holds a Suppleme same time hold this Book.

4. It is a summary offence pu both, for any person—

(a) to obtain a supplementary rati
(b) to apply for or to hold more th
(c) to retain a supplementary rati
(d) to use a supplementary ration
(e) to use the supplementary rat that person, or to lend or gi
(f) to purchase more than the pro wrong periods;
(g) to use coupons for purcha wrong periods;
(h) to deface a supplementary rati

or otherwise to contravene any of thes Order, 1918, under which this book is is

5. For other instructions applica 7 and 8 on your ordinary Ration

N.3. WATERLOW BROS. & LAYTO

Opposite page
Child's, adult's, and supplementary ration books from the second issue of October 1918. Unlike the first issue (of July) the adult's and child's cards had the holder's name and address on the front.

Right Boys converting their school football field to food production, under the stern eye of their headmaster.

named with the relevant commodity. Once again, children under six received half the adult meat ration, which was around 1 lb. of meat, and had books with green covers, as opposed to the buff adult version. Everyone received 6 ozs of butter and/or margarine, 8 ozs sugar, 4 to 8 ozs bacon and ham, 1½ ozs cheese, 1½ ozs tea and (later) 2oz lard. Boys between the ages of 13 and 18, and heavy workers received pink or blue supplementary ration books, giving extra rations.

Rationing did not finish with the end of the war; meat continued to be rationed until late 1919; butter until May 1920, and sugar until November 1920.

Early in 1915, thoughts turned to home food production to bolster supplies, and newspapers gave advice on growing vegetables in the garden.

Allotments increased food production without adding to the labour-shortage as they used 'spare time' labour, and gave everyone a chance to help the War Effort. In May 1916, the Daylight Saving Act (see page 62) made it easier to work on allotments in the evenings. In February 1917, local councils were given powers to seize land lying idle for use as allotments. What became known as 'Allotmentitis' swept the country; lectures and exhibitions of produce with prizes for the best plots increased the interest and success of gardeners locally. Schools created allotments for their pupils on their playing fields. To encourage allotment growers to produce as much as possible, the food hoarding order did not apply to home-grown food.

Keeping animals was also encouraged; 'Woman's Magazine' in April 1917, ran an article on keeping poultry. 'The Scout' in

Photographing the first Potato.

OUT FOR VICTORY.

THE ALLOTMENT HOLDER.
Too old to fight, but doing his bit to beat the U boats.

Above left His first potato – many allotment holders had never grown anything before, and were rightly proud of their efforts.

Above right Working on allotments became a national pastime, with many growing potatoes.

April advised growing mustard and cress to feed chicks. Alternatively; *'If you can get permission, keep a few rabbits on your allotment'.*

The Women's Institute was formed in 1897 in Canada. Its aim was to educate rural women, and to encourage them to get involved in increasing the food supply. Its first meeting in the UK was in 1915 in Wales and the movement grew rapidly. At regular monthly meetings, experts gave talks on subjects such as the bottling, drying and storing of vegetables and fruit, fuel economy, poultry and rabbit keeping, and demonstrations of hay-box cookery, soup and bread-making. Lectures were just the start; ideas were taken up energetically, through the interchange of recipes, produce displays and competitions. WI branches often linked up with local Land Girls, to give them a social outlet.

Above An allotment holder's card from West Ham Park, 1918.

At the outbreak of the war there were between 450,000 and 600,000 allotments in England. By early 1918 there were over 1,400,000, and by the end of the war there was an estimated one plot for every five households.

Chapter 6

Home

Edwardian Britain was a place of greater extremes of wealth and poverty than today. The rich owned grand houses -- often several – during the war many were turned into hospitals or convalescent homes. Housework such as washing clothes and dishes, sweeping and dusting, was done by hand. This required an army of servants; in 1914 the servant population of the UK stood at one and a half million; even middle-class homes had one or two 'domestics'. As the war went on these numbers fell drastically as servants found more independence and better money working in industry. There were few labour-saving or other devices around the house. Most homes were lit by gas, although many still used candles or oil lamps. Heating was usually by coal fires.

Air Raids

In October 1914, with the threat of raids, orders for restricted lighting, called 'dimming', were introduced along the east coast and other perceived targets, including the greater London area. Streetlights were to be put out at 11 p.m., residents had to keep blinds drawn and lights screened; bonfires were forbidden after sunset. The rules were further tightened in November.

With the first bombing deaths in January 1915 people began to take lighting restrictions

We're keeping things going!

ZEPP. BLINDS in accordance with the new lighting regulations. We supply the correct blind in art green special opaque material, 32 in. wide by 2 yds. long. 2/6 Carriage Paid. All widths up to 60 ins.

CATESBYS, London, W.

seriously. Warning systems were set up in places most likely to be attacked. These were often in the form of maroons fired by the police, factory sirens, whistles or hooters. On hearing them, people were to go to the cellar and stay there till the raid was over. In blocks of flats, they should go to a lower floor. Anyone without access to a cellar at home might go to the basement of a nearby shop, factory or church crypt. Tunnels, including, in London, the Underground were also recommended.

In mid-1915 lighting restrictions were extended to cover the whole of England, except for the six most western counties. In May 1915 there were fears that poison gas might be dropped from Zeppelins. Official advice was to keep all windows closed in a raid. Other suggestions included keeping home fires blazing, to burn the gas away. By the end of the month, demand for respirators was such that the shops sold out.

Above Painting by Walter Bayes of shelterers in at the Elephant and Castle underground in 1918, mostly women and children.

Left In a raid, you were advised to go to your cellar if you had one, or to buildings with large cellars such as this one.

Top right Nurses being trained in fire-fighting using extinguishers, buckets, and a form of stirrup pump.

By June complaints about the absence of clear instructions to the public, encouraged others presenting themselves as experts to give, often contradictory, advice. One told people to go to a cellar, while another advised on no account to do so, to avoid being buried alive. Keep your fires blazing, said some, while others advised damping them down, as a fire risk.

In mid-June the police in London issued instructions that people should keep water and sand handy and close all windows and doors on the lower floor to prevent the admission of noxious gasses. Some police advice was obvious, such as not going into the streets during raids, and in particular; 'leave bombs alone — no bomb of any description should be handled'!

Respirators were not thought essential: *'the Commissioner is advised by competent experts that in all probability a pad of cotton waste contained in gauze to tie round the head and saturated with a strong solution of washing soda would be effective as a filtering medium for noxious gases, and could be improvised at home at trifling cost. It should be damped when required for use and must be large enough to protect the nose as well as the mouth, the gauze being so adjusted as to protect the eyes.'*

After October 1915, every building had to have dark blinds or have its lights shaded so that no light emerged, from half-an-hour after sunset to half-an-hour before sunrise. When a raid was imminent, electric and gas supplies were reduced, so the electric and gas lights would dim to a dull glow. This was a warning that aircraft were approaching, and

When there's light in the eyes and light in the heart,
What does it matter if streets are dark!

Above Lighting regulations meant dark streets – the source of romance, but also of accidents and confusion.

Right After the German gas attacks at the front, there were fears of similar attacks by Zeppelin.

THE OLD FORMULA.

Wife. "Look, George—my new respirator."
George (preoccupied). "Oh! By Jove—yes! Suits you devilish well, my dear."

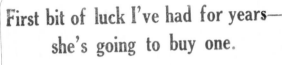

Above left In spite of some reports of panic, the fact that comic postcards were produced showed that not everyone was in a frenzy over possible gas attacks.

Above right One form of air raid warning was policemen carrying placards like this blowing their whistles or shouting "Take cover".

that householders should immediately extinguish lights. No matches were to be struck, nor lights of any description shown, on streets. The results were extremely inconvenient. Streets became tunnels of blackness on moonless winter nights; there were frequent accidents: people collided with trees, posts, and each other. Later, low-power torches were allowed.

In May 1917 the Germans began attacks from twin-engined aircraft. The move from nighttime Zeppelin raids to daytime aeroplane raids brought fresh demands for warnings. In July a new system was introduced in London; warnings given by maroons were supplemented by policemen blowing whistles or sounding horns, and constables on foot, bicycles, or cars shouting 'Take Cover'. The 'All Clear' was to be sounded by bugles – and calls went out for buglers to help; police stations were swamped by hundreds of boys. In March 1918 the Home Secretary finally authorised the use of maroons at any hour of the day or night.

Fuel Rationing

Factories were working full strength. Many thousands of miners joined up and there was a serious shortage of coal. Consequently prices soared, and energy savings became necessary. One successful answer was the introduction of Daylight Saving, or British Summer Time. This was introduced on 21 May 1916, when clocks were put back an hour to increase the hours of light available early in the working day. With autumn came the slogan; 'Keep the Home Fires Burning Low'.

Fuel was rationed in July 1918. It applied to all coal, gas and electricity used in the home. The amount you got depended on the number of rooms in your house, not counting the scullery, bathroom, cellar, etc., and your location; more was allowed in the north. Additional fuel was allowed if more than six people lived in a home.

Hoarding was out - no consumer could have more than a year's allowance of coal in stock; any excess could be seized. Meter readings had to be taken at least once a quarter; if the allowance was exceeded, the gas or electricity company had to report this to the local Fuel Overseer who could cancel the consumer's supply of coal, or prosecute them.

HINTS ON ECONOMY—
Cut Down Coal.

Above In 1918, fuel rationing was introduced and economy had to be practised.

Economising

In June 1916 the War Savings Committee advised that the rise in prices affecting so many items could only be checked if the better-off bought less. Advice to a house with several servants was that more of the baking and washing should be done at home, and two of the younger maids let go to take the jobs of men called up. Baking at home saved several shillings a week in an average household, and relieved the pressure on bakers who were short-handed both for baking and delivery.

Net curtains, except where necessary for privacy, should be taken down and those used should be washed at home. Home laundering was recommended for men's soft shirts, soft and simple dresses, blouses, and underwear. Starched and ornamental lingerie should be put aside for the duration. These measures would save soap and transport, as well as labour and money.

Christmas

Christmas 1914 was a sober affair. The casualty lists and uncertainty for the future ensured that. However, shortages had, on the whole, not yet begun to bite. Children's presents often showed a patriotic theme. War-related books, toy soldiers and nurses uniforms were popular choices. For some there were Christmas cards from relatives fighting in France.

By 1915, food was becoming expensive, and shortages were having an effect. A few people cut down some items, but all except the poorest celebrated a traditional Christmas. By 1916, however, the Food Controller was frowning on 'Christmas dinner as usual.'

By then food shortages were affecting everyone; pre-war, we imported much of our poultry. Now the price of turkeys, geese, and chicken rose sharply. An article in 'the War Illustrated' that Christmas, said; *'My children will keep the season as a Church festival, and I shall try to make it as bright as possible for them, but as far as extra food is concerned they most certainly will get nothing more than a slightly richer pudding than on usual days with "a fire round it," but I am afraid that there will be no crackers and no snapdragon. The bread and the cakes will be made of war flour, and baking-powder and egg substitutes will take the place of eggs in the cakes; almonds and raisins and chocolates and sugar icing will be things of memory only, though I do think that we may manage a few chestnuts and oranges.'*

Alcohol was frowned upon - something which should be given up for the war. Decorations were mainly natural: sprigs of holly and ivy gathered wherever they grew.

By Christmas 1917 'The Daily Mirror' reported that, in the poorer districts, small dealers were selling turkeys and chickens in quarter cuts -- a novelty at that time. But at least it reported 1917 to be the best year for holly in a long while.

I hope you've watched your coal for Xmas, and not come down to this!

Above One of the dangers of the reckless use of fuel under rationing!

Above Embroidered postcards, made in France and sold to the 'Tommies' serving there. Many were sent to friends and family in Britain, including Christmas versions.

The Ministry of Food came out with recipes, for a 'patriotic menu'. This offered rice soup, filleted haddock, roast fowl, and plum pudding with caramel custard.

Local children's parties were popular. The Food Controller wrote that all entertainments that led to unnecessary eating, particularly of breadstuffs, should be discouraged. *'Such entertainments fall naturally into two classes – those in which amusement is the main consideration, and refreshments are merely incidental, and those in which a good meal for the poor is the main object. In the first case refreshments should as far as possible be entirely dispensed with; in the second the food provided should consist as far as possible of non-essential foodstuffs, and care should be taken to avoid those articles of which there is a temporary shortage, such as tea.'*

Above Packing a Christmas parcel for Daddy. A scene repeated
many thousands of times throughout the country.

Pattern No. 8088.   Pattern No. 8089.   Pattern No. 8090.

Sizes medium and large.

Above Pinafores and overalls, from Woman's Magazine of June 1917. Good wages in the factories tempted more and more domestic servants into industry, and increasingly better-off women had to fend for themselves – the overall or pinafore became a must, and a sign that you were 'doing your bit'.

Chapter 7

Clothing

The outbreak of war had major effects on fashion. Pre-war, well-to–do women would change their clothes several times a day, and dressing for dinner was the norm even when dining at home. Lady's maids, whose sole job was to look after their mistress' wardrobe, were among the first to leave for better paid work and a more independent life in the factories.

As women took on war work, they needed more practical clothes. Skirts widened, and long jackets replaced short styles. As men changed into military uniforms, so military-style detailing was applied to women's suits and coats. Khaki became the popular colour.

Only the better-off could afford to keep up with high fashion. Many working-class women and girls made their own clothes, and the cheaper magazines for women were full of free patterns.

In 1915, the typical woman's suit was of military style, a tight-waisted tunic with a full, mid-calf skirt. Popular materials were serge and velvet in dark colours, very plain with little decoration, mainly braiding. Hats were small and close-fitting.

In the autumn, there was a good deal of discussion about a 'standard dress' for women. Suggestions included a riding habit style, with a bowler hat. One correspondent wrote to the 'Daily Mirror' that August commenting, *'It might be monotonous, and in some cases unbecoming; but anything suits a pretty girl, and a plain woman never looks nice in*

Above and right
Motoring outfits 1914. Only the rich could afford any sort of car; many who did would also have a chauffeur.

"MINERVA."
Practicable coat for motoring with adjustable collar, made in check tweeds with belt across back, half-lined satin .. **5¼ Gns.**

Some Pretty Scarf-Trimmed Hats

anything.' Many commentators agreed that while a standard dress was impractical, there might be a standard costume for boys up to age 17, along the lines of a boy scout uniform. This would be shorts, a shirt, jersey, and long socks.

In 1916 the move away from the Victorian hour-glass shape continued. Dresses, often in jersey, lost their waist, hanging loosely straight down from the shoulders.

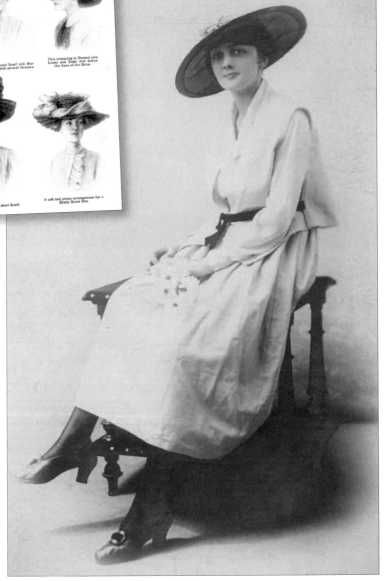

Above Fashionable hats were big in 1917, these from Woman's Magazine, May 1917.

Right Early-war summer dress, the long hem-line gives the date, and shoes, instead of boots, the season.

Opposite page Women's suits from 1915. Cloth shortages had not yet begun to affect the length of the skirts. These were not for everyone – at 7½ guineas, the model on the right was almost a month's wage.

YOUR SUIT

We can give you extra special value owing to advantageous purchases of cloth. We arrange very easy terms and *guarantee* perfect fit and absolute satisfaction. Write for Style, Book, Measure Form, and Patterns for examination.

Above The cut of men's suits changed little over the course of the war, narrow trousers with turn-ups, long jacket, buttoned high, with a full, slightly winged, collar. The straw boater was popular in summer, and the bowler always acceptable.

Right In mid-war the most fashionable 'bright young things' assumed an alarming 'T'-shaped silhouette, consisting of a ridiculously restricting 'hobble' skirt, and an enormous hat.

The three-quarter-length suit jacket was most fashionable, especially in corduroy, serge or broadcloth. The fashion for military-style features continued in the form of epaulettes or gauntlet cuffs. In furs, goatskin was all the rage.

The U-Boat campaign of 1917 seriously disrupted supplies of raw materials such as cotton. Throughout the spring and summer of 1917 cloth shortages increased. Silks and satins had become the most popular materials, due to the scarcity and subsequent high price of wool, which was needed for uniforms. Designers borrowed ideas from men's clothing offering women's versions of waistcoats, gabardine coats, walking canes, and ties, while men's-style hats were popular. Practical colours, such as brown, beige, black, blue and green dominated.

As the casualty figures grew, so mourning dress became common in a restrained form; overt shows were frowned upon. At the same time there was an increase of what were called 'girl knuts', what might later be called 'bright young things'. They wore hobble skirts and thimble hats, or enormous hats; some topped them with clusters of life-size oranges, sheaves of lilies of the valley, or a three feet long wing. Cinema programmes in 1917 carried notices such as *'Ladies who are wearing large hats are respectfully requested to consider the feelings and comfort of those sitting behind them.'*

WHEN NEXT A LETTER YOU SEND TO ME, LET ME HAVE A LITTLE TEA!

Above and below
In 1916 the National Savings Committee issued its famous poster to discourage women from reckless spending on clothes.

In the fashion at last !

A 'standard cloth' was proposed. This was a cheap material for use in clothing for the less well off. At first a single type of cloth would be made available at a fixed price; only broad details governing its manufacture were laid down to introduce 'a reasonably large variety of patterns so as to avoid an undesirable uniformity'. Using this, men's suits could be made and sold at a fixed price.

By 1917 British manufacturers not only supplied boots to the British army, but to the Russian and later, American, armies. The civilian population was at the back of the queue as far as footwear was concerned. This became a source not only of discontent but also a danger to health. In mid-September, a scheme for the production of *'cheaper boots for the multitude'* was announced. For men there was a strong boot for agricultural workers, one suitable for quarrymen and miners and a boot for ordinary town wear – and two each for boys and youths.

By 1918 fabric shortages, especially of wool worsened. No designer could use more than 4½ yards of cloth per suit, dress or coat. A new fashion was for 'shawl-coats' -- old paisley shawls converted into coats. Adaptability was the most important thing in dresses as women began to change only once, or at most twice, a day. The jersey dress and loose coat or tailored suit became the mainstay for most women.

By then a wide range of patterns of standard cloth were available and arrangements made to manufacture 1.2 million yards of it for men's, youths' and boys' suits. The manufacture of three million yards of flannel, and standard blankets was also arranged.

Standard shoes did not appear until January 1918, and then only as samples, so wholesale and retail boot firms could place orders. In an attempt to save materials, 'the High-Legged Boot Order' came into effect in February, prohibiting the sale of women's boots more than 7 in. in height if of leather, or 8 in. in height in other material. Women's agricultural or industrial boots were exempt. At last, in early March, adverts appeared for standard shoes and boots.

Above Mid-war wedding dress; note the raised hemline and the mob-cap style headdress.

Right By the latter part of the war cloth shortages were becoming drastic, and a cheap 'standard' cloth was introduced (somewhat slowly) by the Government.

Talking about standard cloth, how would a nice length of navy suit you?

Right Typical 1917 frock, scandalously short by pre-war standards, worn with high leather boots. In February 1918 an order prohibited the sale of women's leather boots more than 7 in. high or 8 in. in other materials.

Above A hand-knitted 'Golf coat with sailor collar' the instructions for which were given in 'Home Companion' magazine, 10 Nov 1917.

In February the 'National Dress' for women was launched. Designed by Mrs. Hawkey, its main features were that it could be made at home, needed only two-thirds the material used in a normal dress, and used elastic in a combined-belt-and-shoulder-straps harness; different styles or colours of these could be worn over the same dress to produce new outfits.

In June 1918, a travelling exhibition of the new standard clothes for men, standard blankets, flannel and hosiery toured the country. There followed a series of announcements of new standard clothes, including hosiery and standard suits for men and boys, and standard material for women's wear. However there were none available in any shops. At the end of June the Bishop of Stepney said *"The really fashionable clothes to-day, are clothes that have been mended."* As each new production deadline came and went, a few blankets, some cloth and other pieces appeared in shops, but it would be 1919 -- long after the end of the war -- before the clothes arrived in any numbers. When they did arrive they proved unpopular; the dye ran, the material was poor, and the prices high.

Above Woman's shoe from 1917

Right The 'National Dress', as designed by Mrs. Hawkey, was launched early in 1918.

Chapter 8

Doing Your Bit

The nation, especially the women and children, plunged itself into voluntary war work. Much of the effort was organised locally. When people living near military bases and hospitals learnt of shortages of blankets, they organised house-to-house collections. Women washed uniforms in their own homes. In some military camps, women taught elementary cookery, and domestic economy teachers showed soldiers how best to use their rations. From the start of the war, people knitted warm woollen clothing - 'comforts' for soldiers – particularly knitted balaclava helmets, socks and gloves.

Knitting for the troops was popular. Wool advert from April 1916 (right), and 'helmet with cape pieces' (above) from a pattern in the book mentioned in the advert.

NOTHING LIKE HAND-KNITTED SOCKS FOR WEAR AND COMFORT. Make them for our soldiers at the front from J.&J. BALDWINS 5-PLY WHITE HEATHER SCOTCH FINGERING WOOL on the fine recipe given in their booklet No. 17— "Knitted Comforts for Men on Land and Sea," post free for 2½d. on application to—

J. & J. BALDWIN & Partners Ltd. HALIFAX, Eng.

'Flag Day' collectors became a regular sight; women and girls sold miniature paper flags in aid of charities to be worn on the lapel. The first was devoted to Belgian refugees.

One way to support 'the boys' was to send parcels containing food, sweets, tobacco, etc. At first this was to friends and relatives, but collections for local regiments started, while schools and other groups adopted a ship or a unit. In rural areas committees were formed to despatch hampers of cakes and knitted comforts, as well as fruit and vegetables to ships, while others collected books.

Funds were started by newspapers, magazines, or local organisations. Cigarettes were popular and 'Fag Days' were common. The Government acted generously, allowing tobacco

Above and below
Collecting flag (above), and envelope seals sold in aid of disabled soldiers (below).

Opposite page Leaflet promoting the donation of old books for the soldiers and sailors.

to be purchased free of duty for sailors and soldiers (at a quarter of the normal cost), provided it was despatched through recognised trade channels.

Groups such as Queen Mary's Needlework Guild supplied clothing and other necessities, not only to service people, but also soldiers' families, hospitals, charitable institutions, poor parishes, and missions. As with many groups, QMNG members were issued a badge to show the wearer was engaged in regular volunteer work. With the approach of Christmas 1914, a wave of new funds and collections were set up, to provide Christmas dinners, parties or presents for the troops, their families, or other needy groups. In October 1914, Princess Mary launched an appeal to give everyone in the forces a Christmas present in the form of a brass tobacco-box emblazoned with a bust of the Princess. It contained cigarettes, tobacco, and a Christmas card; accompanying it was a silver-mounted briar pipe. As not everyone smoked, alternatives included a packet of sweets, a writing case, chocolate, and a 'bullet pencil'.

The war was only two days' old when the Women's Emergency Corps was established to organise help to deal with emergencies. Their aim was to give assistance to women thrown out of employment. To this end they set up workrooms and organised a considerable industry manufacturing toys. Charities also housed, fed and clothed many of the 265,000 Belgian refugees who came to the country in the first few months of the war, and founded the National Food Fund, the Women's Emergency Corps, the Women's Volunteer Reserve (the first group of women to wear military uniform) and the Women's Emergency Canteens.

In April 1915 poison gas was first used on the B.E.F. at Ypres. The War Office asked the public to help provide the many thousands of gas masks suddenly needed for the army. There were two types, either of which could easily be made. The first was a

BOOKS for SUITE SOLDIERS
AND
SAILORS

Our **Sailors** on the Sea

Our **Soldiers** in Camp and Trench

Our **Wounded** and **Sick** in Hospital

Ask you for Books

Old books, new books, magazines and all kinds of literature needed. We have sent hundreds and thousands of books to them already, but they want more—millions more.

WHAT TO DO

Merely take all the books and magazines you can spare into the nearest Post Office and hand them over the counter, that's all. *They must not be wrapped up and there is no postage to pay.* Collect all the books you can find and

TAKE THEM TO-DAY

Do not decide to take them to-morrow, you may forget; take them *now* while you think of it.

These books go straight from the Post Office to the Camps Library which is a War Office Depôt (or other distributing organizations approved by the Admiralty and War Office), and from thence, without delay, to our gallant men at home and abroad.

Our men are *waiting* for *you* to send them something to read.

You won't disappoint them—will you?

Right and below
Pin-back paper 'flag' sold for the National Egg Collection, and a post card. Such cards show the humour with which many faced the effects of war.

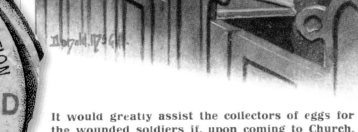

It would greatly assist the collectors of eggs for the wounded soldiers if, upon coming to Church, each lady would lay an egg in the Font!

NATIONAL EGG COLLECTION.
FOR THE WOUNDED
PATRON:
H.M.QUEEN ALEXANDRA.
154, FLEET ST, LONDON.

face piece covering the mouth and nostrils, formed of an oblong pad of bleached absorbent cotton wool, covered with three layers of bleached cotton gauze, held in place with an elastic loop. The second was a piece of double stockinette with a loop of thick plaited worsted at each end to hook over each ear. The response was enthusiastic; local stocks of the required materials sold out rapidly, but by the end of April, public help was no longer needed as industrial production caught up with demand.

Fundraising and collecting 'comforts' went on throughout the war. From July 1915 novels and magazines could be given in at post-offices for distribution to service people. In May 1916 the 'National Egg collection' opened, while prisoner-of-war funds sprang up.

Below Queen Mary's Needlework Guild surgical branch badge, with 1917 and 1918 bars. The branch made hospital supplies including clothing for the wounded.

Right The war was costing millions a day. People were encouraged to invest their money in Victory Bonds and War Savings Certificates.

On January 1 1918 Lloyd George issued a message saying; *"Money is essential to victory. It is, therefore, the duty of all to save what they can and to lend what they can to the community at this time. Every man, woman and child ought to make it a point of honour to increase his holding of National War Bonds as the year goes by.'* Bonds for £5, £20, and £50 were sold through Post Offices, which accrued 5 % interest annually. Alternatively, 15s. 6d War Savings Certificates, would repay £1 in five

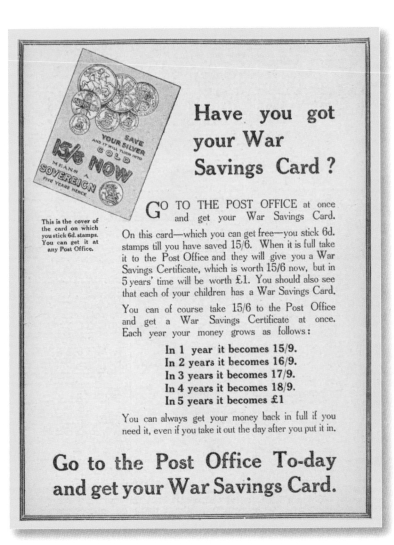

Right The war was costing millions of pounds every day; some of this was raised through increased taxes, while more was raised in the form of war saving certificates, which could be saved up for by collecting 6d savings stamps

years. War Savings Cards had 31 spaces for 6d savings stamps. When the card was full the Post Office exchanged it for a certificate. War Savings Committees were established in workplaces, schools, churches, and clubs. By the spring of 1917 more than 18,000 groups had been set up.

War Weapons Weeks based around local meetings and displays of tanks, aircraft and artillery. Often the stated aim was to collect, say, £5000 to buy a tank.

Plans for dealing with war casualties were based around the military hospitals and the 23 general Territorial hospitals; these were supplemented by reserves of beds in large civilian hospitals, and smaller hospitals organized by the Voluntary Aid Detachments (VADs). Overseas, and later in the UK, hospitals for wounded men run and staffed entirely by women and funded by donations, made a major contribution.

Right Many large country and town houses were converted to VAD hospitals and convalescent homes during the war.

V.A.D. Red Cross Hospital, Standish

Above Trafalgar Square was converted in 1918 into a French village with broken house, ruined windmill, and trench work as part of a 'Feed the Guns' campaign for war savings.

Included among the 724 civil, auxiliary, private, and voluntary aid hospitals in the country were many which had been set up by well-known women, such as one at Woburn Abbey, set up by the Duchess of Bedford. At Brighton the Pavillion was given over for sick and wounded Indian troops, though there only male orderlies were employed. At Brockenhurst, which also dealt with Indian troops, the matron, her assistants and sisters, were all women who spoke Hindustani.

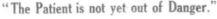

"The Patient is not yet out of Danger."

BLINDED FOR YOU

Above left The large red cross on the front of her uniform shows the nurse to be a VAD. The blue uniform with white facings show the patient to be a wounded serviceman.

Above right Advertisement for St Dunstan's, a charity for blinded servicemen. For some, the wounds would never heal.

The VADs were originally formed for service with the Territorials in the event of invasion. In August 1914, 23 Territorial hospitals mobilised. VADs who wished to do nursing attended lectures; many went through training on hospital wards. There were also VAD pharmacists and cooks. The War Office decided that it would be better for the wounded to be nursed in large military hospitals, so the smaller VAD hospitals were used as convalescent homes. By March 1918 there were over 700 auxiliary hospitals, containing 20,000 beds, the bulk of which were organized and staffed by VADs.

Another voluntary group were the Hospital Supplies Depots, which organised volunteers producing dressings, nightshirts, bedding, and other supplies.

When cotton wool became scarce; appeals were made on behalf of hospitals and casualty clearing stations for sphagnum moss. Work Parties were formed, often of children, to collect, dry, and clean it, before sending it to the hospitals.

Chapter 9

Out and About

DONT
—USE YOUR MOTOR CAR FOR PLEASURE.
—BUY NEW CLOTHES IF YOU CAN MAKE THE OLD DO
—ENGAGE MORE SERVANTS THAN YOU CAN HELP.

I 'm doing my bit !

Transport

Right Posters urged people not to use their cars for pleasure.

In 1914, street lighting was dimmed in many areas as a precaution against air attack. In January 1916, lighting restrictions were introduced for cars and motorbikes. By now petrol was in short supply and posters exhorted: 'Don't Use A Motor-Car For Pleasure.'

Below A head lamp mask made by painting over the lamp glass.

DIAGRAM SHOWING THE ARC OF CLEAR GLASS LEFT ON THE HEAD LIGHT FRONT.

Below Petrol shortages and rationing caused real problems for ordinary motorists.

In May 1916, in several areas, headlights had to be further reduced by covering the whole of the front glass with a disc of cardboard or some other opaque material, with six holes spaced evenly round it. Kerbs and posts were painted white to avoid accidents in the darkness.

In July petrol was rationed and a tax on fuel doubled the cost of petrol to a shilling a gallon. Fuel was rationed by 'Tickets' with 'key workers', such as doctors receiving larger allowances.

Advertised gadgets claimed to improve fuel efficiency; alternatives included mixing two parts petrol with one part paraffin and, in an emergency, gin, whisky, or methylated spirits.

In 1917, coal-gas powered vehicles appeared. Their main drawback was that they used vast amounts of uncompressed gas, so needed a large, flexible bag to hold the gas, and a wooden superstructure to hold the bag. Even then, a full gasbag would only give the equivalent of a couple of gallons of petrol. A pipe was needed for recharging at wayside gas points; in an emergency, the driver could connect to a lamppost. Cars carrying gasbags had to keep below 30mph for fear of the bag flying off, and gas-powered motorbikes were unwieldy. In January 1918 the Board of Trade banned the use of gas for vehicles.

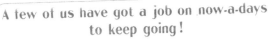

A few of us have got a job on now-a-days to keep going !

GARAGE

NO PETROL OBTAINABLE TO-DAY

Public transport

Public transport was hit by the large number of its workers joining the services while passengers increased by 50%.

In London, when air raids began in 1915, many sought safety in the Under-

Above left A gas-driven car, with its massive gas-bag from 1917. Note also the female chauffeur.

Above right Underground poster from 1915, showing a level of humour we might not have expected.

Below London Motor Buses, painted dull grey green, moving troops and ammunition in France in 1914. The war required a huge increase in military transport.

Right woman conductor (centre), and tram driver (right) in Croydon.

STATIONMASTER (to lady stranded in country station): "WELL, MA'AM, YOU CAN SLEEP WITH THE PORTER!"
OLD LADY: "SIR, I'M A RESPECTABLE MARRIED WOMAN!"
STATIONMASTER: "SO IS THE PORTER!"

Above Women took on many roles in public transport as ticket collectors, porters, conductors and drivers, as well as maintenance.

ground; over 80 stations opened outside usual hours as public shelters. These proved popular, with as many as 12,000 sheltering at Finsbury Park and 9,000 at Kings Cross during raids.

On the railways, from the spring of 1916 prominent lights were extinguished when warnings were sounded, and other lights reduced to the absolute minimum by shading or painting. Trains kept running but at no more than 15 mph for passenger trains and 10mph for goods trains. Fire-box doors had to be kept closed, and whistling and blowing off steam limited. From half-an-hour after sunset until half-an-hour before sunrise, carriage blinds were lowered and might be lifted only when the train halted at a station.

The serious shortage of coal early in 1918 meant railway services were further cut. In the London area season ticket prices on the District Railway and the tubes were raised by 10% for distances up to 12 miles and by 20% for longer distances.

Labour shortages meant that by mid-1915 many tram companies reluctantly trained women as conductresses. Men already employed elsewhere volunteered as part-time drivers, but this could not fill the gap, so women were also trained as drivers.

Entertainment

During the war, theatres patronised by wealthy people declined, while popular houses were crowded. Business boomed in music halls and cinemas. A Royal Albert Hall programme, from December 1917, informed patrons that air raid warnings would be given at least 20 minutes before an attack, *'to enable persons who may wish to proceed home to do so'.*

In March 1918 in response to the coal shortage, the board of trade ordered that theatres, cinemas and all other public places of entertainment were to put out the lights by 10.30 p.m.

Music hall

This was the heyday of the music hall; a cross between a variety theatre and a bar. A singer was usually top of the bill, followed by comedians, Pierrot troupes and minstrels in 'black-face', magicians, acrobats, jugglers, escape artistes, animal and 'novelty' acts, and newsreel films. Alcohol-fuelled audiences could be rough on acts they disliked; in shipbuilding towns it was not unknown for artistes to have iron rivets thrown at them. In 1914, in an effort to improve behaviour, the LCC banished drinking from the auditorium to a separate bar.

Music Halls played their part in the war effort, organizing on-stage recruitment, most famously by Vesta Tilley, a male impersonator who earned the nickname "Britain's Greatest Recruiting Sergeant". She would sing popular and patriotic songs such as 'We don't want to lose you (but we think you ought to go)"and "Rule Britannia". As she sang she walked among the audience inviting men to follow her up onto the stage where recruiting officers would sign them up. Children handed white feathers to those who declined. Popular songs included 'Keep the Home Fires Burning' and 'When war has begun we will follow the drum'. George Formby, Senior, billed as 'The Wigan Nightingale', spoke at rallies, while the "Queen of the Music Hall", Marie Lloyd, sang "*I didn't like you much before you joined the army, John, but I do like you, cockie, now you've got your khaki on*".

Above Ernie Mayne, heavyweight comedian, sang of 'Lloyd George's Beer', *"Dip your bread in it. Shove yer head in it. From January till October, And I bet a penny that you'll still be sober."*

Growing casualty lists put an end to the popularity of the jingoistic song, which was replaced by romantic and comedy songs. Those mentioning the war were more thoughtful, such as, "Pack Up Your Troubles", or comic songs such as Ernie Mayne's "Lloyd George's Beer" and "My Meatless day". By 1916 even Vesta Tilley was singing, "I've got a bit of a Blighty one" about a soldier delighted to have been wounded seriously enough to be sent home.

Above Vesta Tilley, on stage dressed as a 'Tommy'.
The male impersonator was an enthusiastic recruiter.

Right Marie Lloyd, the 'Queen of the music hall', sang some of the most memorable, often saucy, songs of the period.

MARIE LLOYD,

One of the most popular piquante Music Hall Favourites.

Ogden's *Guinea Gold Cigarettes*.

Marie Lloyd and Harry Lauder were among the stars who raised money for war charities and entertained troops at the Front in France. Gertie Gitana, dubbed 'the Forces' sweetheart', entertained wounded servicemen in hospitals, as did Vesta Tilley and Marie Lloyd, who also toured munitions factories. Local entertainers featured too in the concert parties which were a feature of life in military hospitals.

Right The grand patriotic spectacular was a particular feature of the music hall in the early years of the war. This one from 1915.

LITTLE EMMIE.

PAULINE RIVERS.
GRAND SPECTACULAR BALLET.
FOR LOVE OF MOTHER COUNTRY.
THE TOWER BLACKPOOL. 1915.

PHOTO BY.
J.P. BAMBER.
BLACKPOOL.

ALL THIS WEE[K]

OFFICIAL WAR FILM

The Battle of
The Somme

FIVE REELS

" If the exhibition of this Picture all over the world does not end War, God help civilisation ! "—
Mr. Lloyd George

"THE BATTLE OF THE SOMME." is the greatest moving picture in the world—the greatest that has ever been produced. A great war picture, it is the finest peace picture the world has ever seen ; it is worth a thousand Hague conferences. Wherever it is shown it should make an end in the minds of men to the pretensions of pompous princes who have too long claimed the right as the "All Highest" to doom their fellow-creatures to suffering and destruction for the gratification of their mad ambitions. It is impossible to believe that the world will ever forget this picture ; its impression will never fade from the memory of this generation. Men who see it will never lightly talk of war again. In this picture the world will obtain some idea of what it costs in human suffering to put down the devil's domination."—*London Evening News.*

The HAVELOCK
PICTURE HOUSE.

Fawcett Street : : Sunderland.

Continuous Performances from 2.30
Orchestral Music. Cafe Open from 11 a.m. daily.
Admission Prices (including Tax):
4d. 7d and 1 :

Above A newspaper advert for the film 'The Battle of the Somme', from 1916. In this, and other films, people could, for the first time, see moving pictures of the fighting at the front.

Cinemas

Cinemas were a new form of entertainment. The first newsreel films from the front showed troops training, relaxing or playing football. People soon tired of these, wanting film of the action. In 1916 the War Office released 'The Battle of the Somme' a full-length documentary and propaganda film shot by Geoffrey Malins and John MacDowell, two official cinematographers. This showed soldiers 'going over the top', falling back dead or wounded, stumbling through the wire, and being carried on stretchers. Much of the actual battle footage was shot from a long distance or staged. By January 1917 the Daily Mail had a full-page advertisement headed 'Come And See The Tanks Advance At The Front.' *'Take the wife and children,'* said the announcement, adding, *'Nothing faked.'*

Sport

In May 1915 the government asked the Jockey Club to suspend all race meetings, except New-market. When war was declared the cricket authorities cancelled all matches for the duration - people were outraged that football did not follow suit. In parliament it was suggested that football grounds be commandeered for military purposes. Matches continued throughout the 1914-15 season and the FA Cup took place as normal, although many footballers had joined up. At the end of the 1914-15 season, the League suspended its programme for the rest of the war.

Above Women's football team from Portsmouth. Many men's teams were hit by players joining the forces; large crowds began to attend women's matches.

In many munitions factories, sport, especially football, was encouraged as a healthy recreation for their women workers. Factories formed their own ladies' teams. The most famous of these was Dick Kerr Ladies from Preston. Founded in 1917, their matches drew massive crowds, often more than had attended men's matches, pre-war.

Eating out

From December 1916, no more than three courses could be served in any public eating place between 6 p.m. and 9.30 p.m., or two courses at any other time.

Soon after, the Ministry of Food introduced five potato-less days a week. Cafes and restaurants could not serve potatoes except on Wednesdays and Fridays. Going out for afternoon tea was discouraged from mid-April 1917: no public eating place could serve an individual customer more than 2oz. in total of bread, cake, bun, scone, and biscuit, nor could they be charged more than sixpence for a meal between 3 p.m. and 6 p.m.

A new order fixing the average amounts of food to be served to each customer, came into operation in April. In September four 'National Kitchens' were trialled in London, offering meals of good, non-shortage foods such as vegetable soup, fish pie and baked rice at low prices. They proved popular enough to be copied in other cities.

Good gracious! you haven't been in a raid, have you?

Oh no! they had some beer at the Red Lion, and I tried to get in!

Above Beer production was more than halved, leading to shortages, and pubs ran dry.

Right Government beer, better known as 'Lloyd George's Beer' was markedly weaker that pre-war beer, to save on ingredients and cut down on drunkenness.

From early 1918, no meat, poultry or game could be served in any public eating place between 5 a.m. and 10.30 a.m., or at any time on meatless days. (This order was revoked in mid-May 1918 after rationing made it irrelevant.). At the same time, excepting children under 10, no milk could be served in a public eating place as or as part of a beverage except with tea, coffee, cocoa or chocolate. No sugar could be supplied except that used for cooking purposes. Between 3 p.m. and 5.30 p.m, no meal could be served containing more than 1½ oz. of bread, cake, bun, scone and biscuit.

Drink

Alcohol was a problem; brewing used valuable grain and sugar, while a major increase in drunkenness among men and women affected industry. In January 1915 Lloyd George started a campaign, asking people to pledge that they would not drink alcohol during the war. In April the King announced that the Royal household had taken the pledge.

In 1915 too, the Government cut licensing hours, watered the beer and prohibited people buying drinks 'on the slate' or for others ('treating').

Pre-war beer production of 36 million barrels was gradually brought down to just over 16 million barrels and the supply of spirits reduced by 50%. At the same time, prices and tax on alcoholic drinks increased.

London's opening hours - formerly 5am to half past midnight, had been cut to noon to 2.30 pm, and 6.30 to 9.30 pm. Most rural areas took no notice of these new restrictions.

Early in July 1917, Bonar Law announced that more beer was to be brewed, but considerably weaker than before. It was officially known as Government Ale, but more commonly called Lloyd George's Beer. Spirit drinkers fared little better: by April 1918 a bottle of whisky cost £1, five times its pre-war cost.

LIQUOR CONTROL BOARD

NEW BEER

BAD AS YOU ARE I WANT YOU.

The Time for Flags

THE end of the war will be the time for flags— the end of the war will also herald the return of

SUNBEAM

cars, the post - war models being standardised upon the experience we are gaining to-day. They will be worth waiting for.

THE SUNBEAM MOTOR CAR CO., Ltd.
Wolverhampton. Manchester : 112, Deansgate.

Agents for Cars for London and District :
J. KEELE, LTD., 72, *New Bond St.,* W.

Dunlop Tyres are fitted to Sunbeam Cars as standard.

A HAPPY CHEER
NOW IT'S HERE !

Chapter 10

Peace

Early in October 1918, the German Chancellor asked for an Armistice (ceasefire to discuss terms). Austria and Turkey asked to be included. Germany was bankrupt and on the verge of revolution. On 9 November the Kaiser abdicated and fled to Holland. At five o'clock on the morning of Monday, 11th the Armistice was signed; hostilities were to end at eleven o'clock. In Britain, the Prime Minister announced the news at 10.20; church bells rang, and schools and shops were immediately closed. News-papers published special editions, but the presses could not print them fast enough for the crowds that quickly gathered.

For many, especially those mourning dead friends or relatives, jubilation seemed inappropriate. In London the maroons which had heralded air raids were sounded at eleven o'clock and all over the capital men and women climbed on to cars or commandeered buses to go to the centre. At Bucking-ham Palace, the King repeatedly waved to the crowds from the balcony, illuminated in the evening by stage lights. He had kept his pledge to abstain for the duration; now he celebrated with a bottle of brandy laid down by George IV to celebrate Waterloo. When darkness fell, the crowd danced under the newly turned-up lights in Trafalgar Square. Bonfires were lit. Big Ben, long silenced, rang out and was lit up. In fashionable restaurants peo-ple stood on tables while the music halls were reported to be 'in a state of anarchy'.

Most celebrations were more muted. In Portsmouth, one observer recalled; *'In a few minutes all Portsmouth seemed to be in the streets, cheering, laughing, and crying. As though by the wave of a fairy's wand, nearly every child was furnished with a little flag, either the Union Jack or the Stars and Stripes, and, actuated by one impulse, there was a general move to Town Hall Square.'* At St Austell, an attempt was made to dance the traditional Floral Dance, but few could recall the steps and in any event the streets were too crowded. After years of light-ing restrictions, many celebrated that evening by turning up the lights in every room, and opening the curtains, and many went to church. The following Sunday, 17 November, was observed all over the kingdom as a Day of Thanksgiving.

Above A young lady in her Victory costume.

Left Adverts, like people, looked to the end of the war, and a return of normality.

Right Many local authorities celebrated peace by giving out, especially to schoolchildren, commemorative peace medals, such as these from Bethnal Green.

Spanish flu had arrived on the eve of victory; it came in three waves. It first struck in spring 1918 in northern naval ports; a second wave reached its climax around the time of the Armistice, and a third early in 1919. Schools, cinemas and offices were closed; streets were sprayed with chemicals and people devised their own anti-germ masks. People bought remedies and protectives – most of them useless. In some workshops smoking was allowed in the belief that the fumes were germicidal. The death toll in Britain was between 150,000 and 200,000; soldiers were to be seen hastily making coffins and digging rough graves, an exercise with which they were all too familiar. The saddest deaths were those of servicemen who had survived the war only to die from the flu, among them Captain Leefe Robinson, who had shot down the first Zeppelin at Cuffley.

On Saturday, 28 June 1919 the Versailles Treaty was signed. At 6 o'clock that day the roar of the first gun crashed out in London, announcing peace, and the cannonade which followed was heard as far away as Hornchurch in Essex. Saturday, 19 July was proclaimed as a Bank Holiday to celebrate Peace. That day, in London there was a 'Grand Victory March' with nearly 15,000 troops taking part, led by Allied commanders. Thousands of spectators lined the route.

Outside the capital, smaller parades took place, as well as other commemorative events over the course of the following week. In Crieff, Scotland, householders were asked to decorate

Opposite page, left William Leefe Robinson, hero of the Cuffley Zeppelin, survived being shot down and a German prisoner of war camp, only to be a victim of the Spanish flu'.

Price
SIXPENCE

COUNTY BOROUGH

OF SOUTH-AMPTON

1914   The Great War   **1919**

Peace Celebrations

Right Programme of Southampton's peace celebrations, July 1919.

Official Handbook and Programme of Events
19th, 21st, 22nd, and 26th JULY, 1919

their homes, and bonfires were lit. Children's sports the following Wednesday were accompanied by the music of the band of the Black Watch. In Hornchurch, on the Thursday afternoon, 1,450 children were provided with free teas, and were entertained with sports, including races, and a football match. Elderly people were given tea parties.

With the anniversary of the Armistice approaching, on 6 November 1919, the King published a message to the nation, *'it is my desire and hope that at the hour when the Armistice came into force … there may be, for the brief space of two minutes, a complete suspension of all our normal activities. During that time, except in the rare cases where this may be impracticable, all work, all sound, and all locomotion should cease.'* This was the start of the Remembrance Day tradition. It continued for many years before it was transferred to the Sunday nearest to the 11th, only to be revived on 11 November at the end of the 20th century.

All the tribulations of the home front seemed as nothing to those of the troops, whose experiences were recorded and retold, while those of the civil population were all but forgotten. Hopefully this book will go a little way to redressing that.

Acknowledgements

As ever, I should like to thank Ian Bayley, my publisher, for being such a dream to work with, my wife Carol without whose help and support I would never have been able to write a single book. I must also thank our designer, Phil Clucas, whose excellent design, carried out quickly and calmly, has turned chaos into harmony. Finally, I have to thank my sons William and Ralph, and Ian's family; Jan, Michael and Charlotte, without whose patience none of this would have proved possible.